Winter Sleep

Bibliotheca Iranica
Persian Fiction in Translation Series
No. 2

Previously published title in this series includes
No. 1
The Patient Stone
A Novel By
Sadeq Chubak
Translated from the Persian By
M.R. Ghanoonparvar
ISBN:0-939214-62-8

Winter Sleep

Goli Taraqqi

Translated from the Persian by
Francine T. Mahak

Mazda Publishers
Costa Mesa, California
1994

Library of Congress Cataloging-in-Publication Data
Taraqqi, Guli.
    [Khvab-i Zamistani. English]
    Winter Sleep/ Goli Taraqqi; translated from the Persian by
    Francine T. Mahak.
            p. cm. — (Persian Fiction in Translation; No. 2)
    I. Title. II. Series.
    PK6561.T2835 1944
    891'.5533—dc20   94-8737
                                                         CIP

Author's photograph is by Maryam Zandi, Tehran. Reprinted from
Stories From Iran edited by Heshmat Moayyad, courtesy of Mage
Publishers, Inc., Washington, D.C. Copyright © 1991.
Cover design by Farzaneh Foroughi.

ISBN:0-939214-42-3

انتشارات مزدا

Winter Sleep is one of very few Iranian novels written by a woman, who is also a non-engagé writer. This novel takes us into the private world of the individual as he struggles with the "modernization" of his society—a process that most of us in this century have experienced, but that in developing countries has approached the frenetic and the absurd. The picture Goli Taraqqi presents is deceptively simple, and yet we see the tragedy of the individual's stagnation within the empty shell of his uprooted culture. What grips us as readers is the connection we experience with these individuals, whether we feel recognition or disbelief, whether the experiences we share with them are trivial, fantastic, or hilariously human. The mirror reflects and then distorts, but is still a mirror: How would *we* fare if we were abruptly deprived of our cultural bearings?

Winter Sleep's portrayal of personal disorientation in a westernizing society offers a most interesting and unusual interpretation of the individual Iranian experience, with insights that continue to be relevant today. Taraqqi's representation of the psychological effects of western-style modernization on a third-world country is also of interest well beyond the boundaries of a particular nation or culture.

There are significant works in modern Persian fiction which have addressed the problems of modernization and westernization in Iran mainly from a sociological or socioeconomic perspective. Taraqqi's focus is on the individual's inner stagnation, on his private confusion and alienation, which ironically tighten his anguished dependence on his peer group and stunt his psychological and spiritual growth. The images are haunting, yet very real.

The foundation of Taraqqi's psychological portrayal is unique in Persian literature in that it is Jungian rather than Freudian. The symbolism is rich and eloquent: it reveals each main character's inner drama in response to the call to self-realization, as well as his ultimate failure to take on this challenge and mature into adulthood.

Goli Taraqqi experienced the contradictions and superficiality of modernization first-hand during her childhood in Iran, as she sought to integrate the westernized ways of her maternal relatives with the culture and beliefs of her veiled paternal aunts from Qom. She studied in the United States and the University of Tehran, worked for nine years in the government's Plan and Budget Organization, and later taught courses in philosophy as well as myth and symbolism at the University of Tehran. She now lives and writes in France.

F.T. Mahak
Salt Lake City, Utah

1

The wind is blowing in from somewhere, from gaps around the window frames, from under the door, from some invisible crack. Winter is here. It's come back so soon. We used to be all together during the winter—me, Hashemi, Anvari, Azizi, Ahmadi, Mahdavi, and of course Mr. Heydari.

How quickly it passed. Seventy-five years, or maybe seventy-seven, or more. I don't know; I've lost track of the days and the years. A couple of years more or less—who cares? When did old age begin? When did death confirm its presence?

One day someone said: "Watch out old man, be careful not to fall!" I looked behind me. "Yes," I said, "watch out, don't fall!" I looked behind to take the old man's hand, whoever he was, and was shocked. "Does he mean me? " I wondered. I didn't believe it, and went on my way.

Mr. Heydari used to say: "Hey, we have forever until forty. We're not turning forty anytime soon—maybe not for a century. Maybe forty will never come, ever!"

It's so cold. Such a cold wind. The world is freezing over. The world is slowly dying along with me. I turn on the light, put my chair right next to the heater, sit down and wrap the blanket around me.

I wish it were still summertime. I wish we were all still together. What happened? What became of us? As Asgari used to say: "We all belong to each other." And being together was so easy; we never even gave it a thought. Whose fault was it?

Heydari said: "Friends, the secret of our success is in our sticking together. All of you give me your money, and I'll take care of it for you."

Jalili said: "You all make me sick, the things you do, the things you think, the inane things you wish for."

Anvari said: "I think Jalili's just kidding us. It's all a game. His seriousness is just a put-on."

But he was telling the truth. And he did it so easily.

What an awful night it is. What a cold, dark, long night. It's still only seven-thirty. If only Time would stop for an instant, just give us a chance.

I said to myself: "If I shatter my watch, if I close the curtains and shut the doors and windows, then this accursed, stubborn Time will leave me alone." It was a futile thought.

My own heart counted the moments, and with each beat confirmed my continuous advance toward death.

I wanted to believe that death is not the end. I wanted to escape the grip of Nothingness that stands day and night outside my window, watching me. That was even more futile.

I tell myself: "Old man, this time if you catch a cold, you'll die." What precautions, what silly thoughts! "Maybe forty will never come, ever!" I look at the dishes lying next to the wall, at the breadcrumbs on the carpet, at the rat sitting in the middle of the room, dazed.

I miss Hashemi most of all. He used to come every day, in the evening, and he would bring his paintings of colorful birds. He'd lay them all out for me and say: "Listen: this one's singing, can you hear it? " He would sit and talk on and on about his curly-haired little wife, his sweet Shirin-khanom,[1] about what she would do, what she would say, about her voice that was like the cooing of doves, about her eyes, each a different color, about her easy laughter and the scent of her body.

I listen: I hear the sound of the door, footsteps, a voice outside the window. Maybe somebody's come to see me. I look around for my cane, for my shoes, my glasses. Who has remembered me? Who? It makes no difference. It makes no difference at all. Even if it's a stranger who came by mistake, I'll let him in and keep him overnight. I can't find that damn cane. I brace myself against the wall, on the edge of the table, on the back of the chairs.

"Watch out, old man, be careful not to fall!" He was talking to me, when I had never even thought of old age!

I open the door, stick my head out and listen. In the hallway, there is only the cold, the darkness and the garbage can that has started to smell. "Who's there?" I call out. "Is anyone there?" Silence. I go to the edge of the stairs and wait. I call out louder: "The door's open. Come on in!" No. There's nobody there. Just like yesterday, and the day before, and the day before that.

Back in the old days, if someone knocked and didn't come in, I knew it was Ahmadi. Heydari used to say: "Listen, guys, we'd be better off not even letting him in. That man can't be trusted anymore." We'd say: "But Heydari-jan,[2] he's our friend! All seven of us grew up together. How could we do that?"

"Yes, it's really hard." said Anvari. "But what can we do? This one person is harming all of us."

Hashemi said: "Whatever you all say."

Mahdavi said: "Whatever Anvari says."

Azizi said: "I have to think about it. I'll tell you later."

I go back to the heater and sit next to it, wrapping the blanket tightly around me. Who would come to see me? And in this cold, on such a dark, snowy night. I turn up the kerosene in the heater. I'm shaking. "Shirin-khanom," I said, "you're always knitting scarves for us, always worrying that one of us might catch a cold. How can you be so nice and sweet and kind?" She laughed, one of her lovely child-like laughs that still rings in my ears, that still echoes in the back of my mind during some fretful dream, and calms me.

3

I wish it were morning. I wish it were again time to smell summer all over the house. I turn on the radio: it's the news. I'm cut off from everything. Somebody has killed his wife; somebody has killed himself; there's been a flood; the war's still going on; a policeman has won the lottery. It's the same old world. I turn it off.

It's twenty minutes to eight. Nineteen minutes to eight. Sixteen minutes, fifteen minutes, twelve minutes, ten minutes, nine minutes, five minutes, eight o'clock sharp. Tonight I want to remember all the eight o'clocks. I want to wonder. I want to look at myself, at all my days, at all my moments. I want to lay out these seventy-odd years one more time all around me and look at them, at all those lost days that—as soon as I'd wanted to look at them, touch them, smell them—had vanished, and vanished so easily, so silently and stealthily.

Azizi once asked: "Would you want to start all over again?"

I realized I wouldn't, I really wouldn't. Start over again for what? To do what? Unless I knew there was some other way, and I know there isn't. At least there isn't for me. If I were to start over a thousand times, I'd still end up right here.

Jalili said: "Of course there is. There are a million ways. You weren't willing. It was easier that way."

"My friends," said Heydari, "it is in your best interest to listen to me. I've found the secret of success in life, believe me."

Azizi said: "I wish I could get away. I wish I could do something."

"I'll go too," I said. "I'll go with anyone who goes."

Heydari said: "My friends, my dear friends, don't be fooled! Don't let such foolishness get a hold of you! Where could you go that would be better than right here? Once a person lets himself get carried away like that, he'll never have his feet on the ground."

"Let's go for a ride." said Anvari. "The city's all lit up; it's a holiday and there's a lottery and games. There are traffic signs everywhere. Let's go and watch; it'll give us a lift."

"Anything you say. " said Hashemi.

What did we ever say? Come to think of it, who were we,

anyway? It was always whatever Heydari said, Mr. Heydari.

"Wait for Ahmadi!" said Shirin-khanom. "Don't leave him alone!"

"No way. " said Heydari. "Leave him behind."

"Come on, Ahmadi-jan," I said. "what's the matter? What are you so afraid of? "

He didn't answer me. He was, as always, aloof and sullen. Even now sometimes I think he's come back. I recognize the sound of his footsteps, the sound of his helpless footsteps that were always running away, never knowing their destination.

Something is tapping against the window. I listen. I guess it's the wind, or the cold, or the weight of the darkness. A big fat rat is gnawing at the corner of the curtain. I wish someone would come and visit me. I wish someone would call to me outside the window. Back then, at least Fatemeh used to come. That wasn't her name. It wasn't Roqiyyeh or Sakineh either.[3] I don't know what it was. Whoever she was, she was nice. She was someone besides me. Someone else. She would come in twice a week, open the curtains, open the windows, shake out the bedding and lay it out in the sun. She'd wash the dishes and straighten my clothes. She smelled so nice; she smelled of the outside, of streets and shops, of ditches and buses. She was present. She was there. She related to me. She was right in front of me. I knew that if I talked she heard me, if I walked she saw me; she knew if I was there or not. She'd talk the whole time, but not to me. She talked to the table and the chairs, to the doorknob and the samovar spiggot, to the broom in her hand and the clothes she was washing. She related to all the things around her, to the bathroom pitcher, the carpet, the icebox, the scissors and the dustpan. She understood their language. She was a part of them. She didn't talk to me. Or maybe she did and I couldn't hear it; I had become hard of hearing. I remember the last day she came. All her hair had been cut off. She sat in the middle of the room and cried. She said her mistress had cut off all her hair and taken it to the hairdresser around the corner to make into a wig. She didn't tell it to me. She told it to the walls and the chairs, to the carpet and the dishes. Then she left and never came back. That was a long time ago, seven or eight years. Now there are only the rats, big gray rats that eat everything, bit by bit.

What a stubborn wind. Where is it coming from? Maybe from the wall around the heater pipe. Tonight I'll go to bed early. I get under the covers and say to myself: "Old man, watch out. If you catch a cold this time, you'll die." I put my hands in my coat pockets. Down in my pocket, among all the junk, there are two or three seeds and a piece of candy. I take it out and put it in my mouth. It's hard and tastes bad. I spit it out. It's one of Shirin-khanom's candies. Her pockets were always full of chick-peas and candy, of colored string and jasmine flowers. I remember the very first day I ever saw her. The door to Hashemi's house was open. Anvari said: "Hashemi has company." We went in. Heydari said: "Well, well, what's going on here? Who is this? Where did this little treat come from?" Shirin-khanom, fully clothed, was taking a dip in the fountain pool. She was holding her face under the fountain and laughing. Anvari said: "Well I'll be darned! She's no bigger than an ant. A big ant." Hashemi was kneeling on the edge of the flowerbed, spellbound, his mouth gaping and his eyes dazed. He wasn't blinking. He wasn't moving. He wasn't even breathing. Asgari said: "She's so cute! You could hide her anywhere. You could put her in your pocket and take her to the office." Heydari said: "First we have to find out who she is, what kind of family she comes from."

Shirin-khanom waved to us. The sound of her laughter and splashing filled the whole courtyard. Hashemi's pet doves were fluttering all around her. She dipped her finger into the water and flicked it at Heydari. She said something that we didn't catch. Her mouth was full of candy. She looked at us happily, as if she had known us for ages. We didn't know what to say. We didn't know what to do. She got out, barefoot and wet, huddled against Hashemi, leaned her head on his shoulder, and whispered into his ear. Heydari said: "How shameless!"

Anvari said: "What if she's a thief?"

Mahdavi said: "We ought to throw her out."

Hashemi, dumbfounded, was looking at her. He couldn't believe it. Very slowly, hesitantly, timidly and with care, he stroked the tip of her hair and her tiny fingers. It was as if he were afraid she might fly off. "She's an angel of mercy," he said. "God has sent her." Heydari drew him aside and asked: "What's her name? Who is she? Who's her family? " He looked at us, transfixed, and shook his head. He himself didn't know. "The door was open. She came in. Like a dove. Like a plant that just sprouts up in your garden. How do I know? She just came in, that's all."

It was Mr. Heydari's birthday. We talked about buying him something nice, a keepsake from his friends. Anvari said: "I'm going to buy him a pair of Melli[4] shoes." Mahdavi said: "Let's buy him something he can use, like a toolbox for his car or a power saw for his garden." Azizi said: "Oh God. Don't tell me it's Heydari's birthday again!" Shirin-khanom brought him a lovebird. She handed him the cage, then cocked her head, as she always did when she was shy. Later she heard that her bird and its cage had been put in the storage room, with a cover over it. Mr. Heydari had said: "It doesn't have a bad voice, but it sings at the wrong times. It's a nuisance." Shirin-khanom was inconsolable. She wept and wanted her bird back. She was becoming ill. Heydari said: "A ten-toman[5] bird isn't worth all this crying. Here, take it back to her. And tell her not to bring me any more surprises. " She didn't, ever again.

It has started snowing, small flakes coming down fast. I pull the blanket up to my chin. I breathe very slowly, so that the cold air in the room won't make me start coughing. I wait for something to happen, to feel hungry at least, or sleepy, to feel something besides the feeling of sitting and waiting.

I can hear the sound of the snow. It's as if it has settled in my head, in my heart, in my eyes.

I tell myself: "Old man, tonight you're finished. Winter is just beginning, and the summer that's supposed to come is ages away."

"Asgari-jan," I said. "what about that trip you were talking about? Aren't you going? Aren't we going to go? "

He was sitting next to his mother. He combed her hair, massaged her shoulders and spoon-fed her.

I said: "It's going to be too late pretty soon. So when? " He said: "She's my mother. What can I do? I must take care of her."

He had lifted her onto his back and was carrying her around. He looked at me: "What would you do if you were in my place. Huh?"

Heydari said: "Life is as logical as two plus two equals four. There are rules to it. A reasonable man is always happy."

I'd better get up and think about dinner, about sleeping, about the bitter cold, about these stubborn rats that have taken over the whole house. I'd better think of tomorrow and all the days thereafter.

1. The word *khanom,* meaning "lady," is a term of respect when it follows a woman's name, as in this context.

2. The word *jan,* used after a person's name, is a term of endearment.

3. Fatemeh, Roqiyyeh and Sakineh are common women's names among religious, rural, and working-class families.

4. Melli Shoes, Iran's national shoe company, mass-produces a large variety of shoes of rather ordinary quality and style.

5. About $1.40.

2

Mr. Ahmadi hesitated before taking the outstretched hand. He forced himself to take it, then smiled sadly. He made an effort to be cheerful, to talk, to shake hands, to introduce himself and ask how everybody was. He tried to laugh louder than everyone else and say what a great joke that was, to nod, look surprised, ask questions, be sympathetic, and give the address of the best ulcer specialist in town. He tried to be calm and to feel that he's here, alive, with other people, that he has an identity, that he isn't afraid, that he's happy and that there's a lot to be thankful for.

Mr. Heydari had said: "That's it; that's the right attitude. There's still a lot to be grateful for."

And Mr. Anvari had said: "Thank God!" And Mr. Mahdavi had sent a letter saying: "You're right. One should always be grateful."

Mr. Ahmadi turned around, and looked with terror. All the faces were unfamiliar. He turned back and ran his hand over the painful stitches on his head. That unexplained burning sensation under his skin had started up again, that hellish burning mixed with infernal secretions that filled all the pores

9

of his skin, and felt like a dark, solid mass. He felt as if a metallic substance had settled at the bottom of his head, at the pit of his stomach, in the sockets of his eyes. He felt as if he were an ancient tree on which the wind-blown dust of a thousand years had settled, and which was bearing the weight of all things, all moments of history, all real and possible events. He thought of his room, his room without sunshine, and of his wooden bed that brought him everything but sleep, of the quilt that was heavier than a mountain and never adapted itself to his body, and of the pillow that would change at night into a desert filled with gravel and thorns. Making it through the night involved a horrifying journey under the earth, through the din of devils and a thousand evil wandering souls, through the wailing of ghoulish winds. And everything was so dislocated and chaotic that it was like Time before creation, and no one and nothing existed, not even God. There was pure absence and pure loneliness, there was nothing but this estranged being, in pain, for whom each moment spelled doom.

He remembered his heater, that was out of kerosene, and the light in the hallway that had burned out. That's where it had all started, from that cold, dark, narrow stairway. The floor had given way under him, and he had tumbled all the way down to the bottom floor—forty-two steps. It had happened unexpectedly, all of a sudden, as in a dream, as in an imaginary moment. Some invisible hand had pushed him. It had knocked him head over heels, and for three months afterwards his leg had been in a cast. And it still hurt. During the night he would feel sharp pains in that leg, as if it were being pierced with needles.

Mr. Heydari had just laughed. The other friends had laughed too. Even kind Mr. Hashemi hadn't believed him. It was just a simple accident: a lot of people had fallen before, and it could happen to anyone. His landlord had testified before all of them: he was there, he saw Mr. Ahmadi's foot slip, and he saw him fall; the same thing had happened to the previous tenant; there was nothing new about it. And that was all there was to it. Nonetheless, Mr. Ahmadi was convinced that this

10

was no accident. He hadn't been careless or distracted or dizzy. And his foot hadn't slipped. But he had fallen. Why? How? Mr. Anvari had laughed too. He had said: "Well, you could have bought a lightbulb and fixed the hall light. You could have been more careful walking in the dark."

Maybe Mr. Anvari was right. But what about that damned rock? That mysterious rock that had come flying through the air, and no one knew why or where it had come from. The sutures on his head still hadn't healed—sixteen stitches. At night they burned, making him miserable. His friends had sympathized: it had been an unfortunate accident, especially since Mr. Ahmadi's leg was still swollen and he hadn't yet gotten over that ordeal. But nonetheless, it was just a rock that had fallen. And a lot of people have been hit on the head by such rocks. As Mr. Jalili had said: "We've been hit on the head too! We've all had that happen. Nowadays even breathing isn't an easy thing." Mr. Ahmadi had accepted it. He'd had no objections. He'd said: "You're right. That rock wasn't aimed at my head. It wasn't aimed at anybody's head. It didn't mean to do anything but fall. It had to fall on someone's head, and I happened to be there. The same would have happened to anyone else who had been there. What difference does it make whether it was you or me? In the end somebody was going to get his head bashed in."

The man sitting next to Mr. Ahmadi laughed. He shook his head and asked: "What do you think? This is really great!" Mr. Ahmadi answered: "Yes, you're right. It's great." Then he shuddered. The man's face looked familiar, with those naive, dumbstruck eyes, that gaping mouth; a blithe creature all decked out in his tie and shoes. He had seen those hands before; he recognized them. These were the hands he had felt against his shoulder that night on the stairs, in the dark. He was terrified of these hands. These were the hands that had hit him over the head with that rock, the hands that were always following him. They persecuted him; they were out to get him. These hands smelled of death; they smelled of domination and conquest. At night they would come after him, in his dreams, in the depths of his weary, agitated mind. Wherever he was he could feel their presence. He would see them behind windows, among the hands holding the guardrail on the bus, amidst hands reaching out for bread at the baker's, or hands waving hello, writing, counting, praying, killing, or wanting to caress.

Even that night at Mr. Heydari's he had seen those hands and had shuddered. Whose were they? Mr. Heydari's, Anvari's, Hashemi's, Azizi's, Asgari's—whose? And that was the night when that strange accident had happened. Mr. Heydari later told him: "It's your own fault. If you hadn't been next to the window the door wouldn't have hit you in the nose. You wouldn't have had your teeth knocked out. Disaster strikes without warning. You should always be prepared for this kind of thing. You should always figure out where there is the least danger, and stay put right there. Why were you standing next to the window? Why did you want to look at what was going on outside in the street? Why didn't the door hit Mr. Anvari in the face? Because he was sitting in front of the TV minding his own business. Why didn't it break Mr. Hashemi's nose? Because he was busy taking care of his flowers and his canaries. Why didn't it hit me in the face? Because I know what's what. I know where to stand. It serves you right. I told you to come and sit and talk, read a newspaper, work on a crossword puzzle, tell your fortune with the cards, drink vodka, or smoke opium. Find something to keep yourself busy. Go to a movie. play the *tar*.[1] In short, my friend, relax. I mean, what's with you? Why are you always so anxious? What's the matter with you anyway?"

Mr. Anvari had said: "Three broken teeth aren't worth all this fuss. You've got ten more. And your nose will heal. You'll get over it."

Mr. Ahmadi had acquiesced. All he'd said was: "Why me? Why should the door have to slam into my face? You were there too. You all stand next to the door or the window sometimes too. But why do I have to be singled out? It's always me! Who is it that has it in for me? Who is my enemy?"

The man sitting next to Mr. Ahmadi started clapping, and

asked: "Do you use that soap too?"

"What?"

The man said: "How many cards did you collect? " Mr. Ahmadi looked at him.

The man asked: "Do you have a match?" Then he signalled to Mr. Ahmadi to be quiet.

The performance of traditional Iranian music had started. The musicians were wearing Achaemenian costumes. The violinist had a cold, and was wearing a thick woollen scarf around his neck; he was sneezing and his violin was screeching. Mr. Ahmadi knew the tambourine player; he was a math teacher; he had tutored Mr. Jalili's son.

The man said: "What a glorious celebration!"

Mr. Ahmadi realized that he couldn't sit still in his chair. He got up, buttoned his jacket, and started to walk away slowly. "Where to? " the man asked. Mr. Heydari turned around. He frowned and nodded to him to sit back down.

Shirin-khanom was carefully watching out of the corner of her eye.

The hall was almost empty. A servant greeted him, quickly gulping down the sugar lump he had in his mouth. "Is there anything I can do for you?"

Mr. Ahmadi nodded and stood, hesitantly. The servant asked: "Was there something you wanted?"

Mr. Ahmadi said: "A glass of water," and realized that he wasn't the least bit thirsty. He said: "No, I don't want it. Never mind. "

"Would you like some cake?"

Mr. Ahmadi said: "Yes, certainly." And he started feeling queasy; he couldn't swallow. He went out and stood next to the window, and drew the curtain aside. He looked out at the snow, at the trees lined up like white-haired old women waiting for death, at the long, dark street, and the lone flickering light in the window of an oldish building on the other side.

He could feel Shirin-khanom's gaze upon him from afar.

They were at Mr. Hashemi's house. Shirin-khanom was

having a *sofre-ye nazr*[2] for him. She had taken his hand and given him some of the rock candy she'd had blessed for him. Mr. Heydari had said: "It's nothing. You'll forget all about it. Man is forgetful. When he's in pain, he moans and groans and wails, but afterwards he forgets all about it. Pain doesn't stay forever; either it goes away or you get used to it."

Mr. Hashemi was sitting on the steps in the courtyard, weaving something. He was upset. Two of Shirin-khanom's doves had flown away, first the female and then her mate. The female had just laid an egg. Mr. Hashemi couldn't understand: "A pigeon never just leaves its egg. It's impossible. What happened? Why did they leave? They had everything here: water, food, a nest. A pigeon doesn't just fly away, unless it senses disaster. But what disaster?"

Mr. Jalili had answered: "Disaster is in the air. It's all around. It's in the water we drink, in the sounds we hear. You can't see it, but it's there. It's more real than you and me."

Mr. Anvari had said: "We'd better not talk about it."

The servant put the plate of cake on the table next to the wall and asked: "Would you also like some tea?"

Mr. Ahmadi looked out onto the street. Someone was standing under an awning, down the street.

The servant said: "Mr. Anvari has gone to a lot of trouble this year. He organized the entire show himself."

Mr. Ahmadi asked: "Do you know that man? The one standing in the street?"

The servant said: "Mr. Mahdavi was a nice person. It's too bad he went to Gorgan."

Mr. Ahmadi wiped the cold sweat from his face with the back of his hand. A biting pain seared the scar on his head, and he felt as if something was clawing inside his chest.

The servant laughed. The sound of applause rose from the reception hall. Mr. Ahmadi let go of the curtain he had clenched in his fist. He stepped back and looked at the servant with terror, asking: "What's wrong with you? Why are you just standing there, staring at me? What do you want?" He had seen that face before. Where? When? The night he had fallen?

14

The day that rock had cracked his head open? Maybe he was just imagining things. Maybe Heydari and Anvari were right when they'd said: "Ahmadi-jan, you're really beginning to go crazy!"

"Would you like a chair?" the servant asked.

Mr. Ahmadi shook his head and went into the men's room. He locked the door and listened. He bent over and looked through the keyhole. The servant had his back to him. He turned on the faucet and put his face under it; he wet his hands and wiped his neck. He heard footsteps, running, the murmuring of the crowd. He opened the bathroom window and stuck his head out. He started shaking and got goosebumps. "Who is that?" he said to himself. "Why is he standing out there under the snow? What is he waiting for?"

He returned to the hall. The servant was standing at the door of the reception hall, watching. Mr. Ahmadi asked him: "What is it? What's going on?"

The servant said: "How lovely!"

Mr. Ahmadi said: "I'm talking about what's going on in the street."

The servant answered: "It's nothing important, sir. He's got nothing to do with us."

Mr. Ahmadi went back to the window and pulled the curtain aside. That man was still there. The snow blurred the contour of his face.

From the reception hall came the sound of cheering and applause. "Come and watch, sir." said the servant. "The best part of the show has begun!"

"Who is that standing under the awning?" asked Ahmadi. "What does he want?"

"What a sight!" said the servant. "It leaves you speechless."

The employees' parade had started. The senior employees in good standing were carrying the company flag. High-ranking officials held framed pictures of the company's products. They were followed by the column of new employees and their families.

Mr. Heydari, Mr. Hashemi and Mr. Azizi were standing,

applauding.

"Now it's Mr. Anvari's turn," said the servant.

The sound of trumpets rang out. The curtain at the front of the reception hall swang open. The employees intoned the company song. Mr. Anvari was standing, framed inside a giant toothpaste tube with flashing lights. He was the spirit of the toothpaste. He wore a crown of different-colored toothbrushes on his head. He spoke of himself as being soft and sweet-smelling, as the enemy of bad breath. He spoke of his unique revolution, of his holy war against gum diseases.

Mr. Heydari was whispering into Mr. Azizi's ear. Mr. Ahmadi went back into the hallway and leaned against the wall. He knew that someone was standing across the street, in the snow, someone with those same, familiar hands. He pulled the curtain aside. He thought he was dreaming and that he had dreamt this dream many times. The street, the snowy night, the lifeless trees, the black, half-finished building, and the shadow at the end of the street: he'd seen all of this before, it was familiar. He opened the door and went out onto the porch. He ran his hand over the snow on the balustrade. The air was coarse and dense. It clawed at his face like a cutting object. Even the snow was heavy and metallic.

It had been snowing that night too, the night he'd been mistaken for a thief. They had beaten him up and torn his clothes, and then had realized they'd made a mistake. He'd forgotten to take his key, and the landlord wouldn't open the door for him. He'd had his back to a policeman and had been searching in his pocket for his spare key, saying: "This is my house! I came without my key. You know me!" Then he had noticed with horror that his hand was being crushed in the policeman's grip. "What are you doing? Why have you grabbed my hand? What do you want? " He'd tried to continue, but a punch in the stomach had cut off his wind. "What thief?" He'd muttered under his breath. "Are you crazy? Why are you hitting me?" He'd bent over to pick up his glasses, and had felt blood running from his nose and just below his eye. He had pounded on the door, calling out to the neighbors for help. He had held his head with both hands to deaden the pain of the blows, saying: "You've made a mistake! Believe me!" Then he'd passed out. For a long time he couldn't see; his glasses had been shattered underfoot. After the incident he was afflicted with dizzy spells; he had constant stomach pains. Mr. Heydari had said: "Yes, I agree. It really was a stupid mistake. This warrants a thorough investigation; fortunately, the law protects people." Mr. Anvari had said: "I think it was your own fault. After all, what were you doing out in the street at that time of night? Why don't you go to bed at nine like the rest of us? You can't blame the poor policeman; I would have been suspicious too. Law and order in our society is more important than just you or me."

"Sir," asked the servant, "are you all right?" Ahmadi gathered a fistful of snow from the balustrade and squeezed it. He rubbed it over his face, on his parched lips. He opened his mouth and wanted to scream. He wanted to kick the wall in. He wanted to do something. He turned around and saw Shirin-khanom standing in the doorway.

Jalili had said: "That's the way it is, pal and it isn't good. The other guy isn't your friend; he's your enemy. He's become your enemy. You have to fight him: either you gobble him up or you get gobbled up."

Anvari had disagreed: "You have to give a little and take a little, agree a little and disagree a little. It's sort of this way and sort of that way. Life is a kind of compromise."

Shirin-khanom was quietly shaking. Her pearl-like teeth were chattering. "Why are you standing out here?" she asked.

The show had ended. Everyone was leaving. Mr. Anvari's voice could be heard from inside; he was happy and congratulating everyone.

Mr. Heydari had invited his friends over to his house. Mr. Hashemi was looking for Shirin-khanom. Mr. Heydari was holding his umbrella over his head, and his raincoat came to his ankles. His gloves, scarf and hat were all assorted.

Ahmadi looked at the shadow standing in the snow and said to himself: "He's waiting for me. He's come after me. I'd better

17

leave with them: I'll hide under Mr. Heydari's umbrella and take Mr. Heydari's arm. Under Mr. Heydari's umbrella the whole world is safe, and Mr. Hashemi's hand will block the rock that's thrown at me. These are my friends, my shield; they'll protect me."

Mr. Heydari was coming down the stairs ahead of everyone. His umbrella scraped the walls. Mr. Hashemi was hurriedly buttoning Shirin-khanom's coat.

Mr. Heydari's car was parked right in front. Even the back windshield had wipers, and he had chains on all four tires.

Shirin-khanom said: "Hurry, let's go!"

Mr. Anvari carried his crown under his arm, and was shaking hands with all the guests. Mr. Ahmadi wiped the snow off his head and started staring at the servant, who was looking at him. No, he wasn't mistaken. These same eyes had looked at him, with the same calmness, the same indifference. He remembered those eyes from the night he'd been beaten up. A window across the street had been open, and someone had witnessed the whole scene from behind it. Someone had stood there the whole time quietly, watching him get beaten. Mr. Ahmadi had called out to him, said hello. "Hey, mister! Kind neighbor, you know me! You know I live here! We've run into each other many times, talked together, asked about each other's health. Please do something!" And those glassy, lifeless eyes had just stared at him. There had been someone else there too, a passerby who had crossed the street and hurried away as fast as he could. And there had been two other people. They had opened the door a crack, and were looking out through it. He could hear their voices. He'd called out to them too: "Hey, you behind the door! Please do something!" The door had slammed shut, and before he fell he'd heard the sound of a key turning in the lock.

"Aren't you going to go? " the servant asked.

Mr. Ahmadi turned toward him. "You know me, don't you? "

The servant looked at him. Everyone had gotten into Mr. Heydari's car. The windshield wipers were quickly clearing

18

off the snow. Everyone was waiting for Mr. Anvari.

Shirin-khanom was waiting at the foot of the steps. She didn't want to go.

The servant turned off the lights in the reception hall. Mr. Ahmadi cried out: "Wait! Don't go!" and ran down to the bottom of the stairs. The servant shouted: "Sir! Your coat! Your hat!"

Mr. Heydari's car took off. Mr. Ahmadi cried out louder: "Don't go! Wait!"

Shirin-khanom waved to him sadly from inside the car. A shadow down the street was standing motionless. The servant was looking at him through the window.

Mr. Ahmadi stood, breathing with difficulty. A strange clamor raged inside his head. His ears were filled with an inner murmur. Snow was getting in his eyes. He could hear the distant sound of the chains on Mr. Heydari's car. Mr. Anvari had said: "It's your own fault; how is it none of these things happen to us? How come there isn't anything or anyone out to get us? "

Mr. Ahmadi turned up the collar of his coat, and tried not to look down the street. "It's still not too late. " he said to himself. "There's still time. I've got to hurry. I've got to get to Mr. Heydari's house. They wouldn't leave me behind. We grew up together. We're old schoolmates. I've got to hurry."

The servant opened the window and stuck his head out. Mr. Ahmadi started off. The snow quickly covered his footprints. The whole city slept. "Which way? " he wondered. He remembered that Mr. Heydari's house was a long way away, and that it would be impossible to get there on foot. He turned around, stole a glance down the street, and shuddered. He walked faster.

Mr. Heydari had said: "There's no room in our car. Come on your own. " Mr. Ahmadi thought: "Maybe there's no room in their house either. Maybe there's no room anywhere for me."

Mr. Azizi had said: "There's nothing we can do. You know

that." Mr. Ahmadi thought: "By the time I get there it will be late. They'll have had their dinner and gone to bed. They'll have turned out the lights and locked the door. How can I wake them up? How can I disturb their peaceful sleep? They might push me down the stairs and break my leg. Or throw a rock at me from the roof. I've noticed how they look at me, how they point at me and whisper to each other. They've gone and left me behind. They're afraid they might catch the same damned curse I have. What do they care what happens to me? "

He stopped. The snow was getting in his eyes, settling on his head, on his shoulders, covering him from head to foot. The lights behind the curtained windows were going out, one by one. The city, like the tail end of a forgotten story, was breathing in the distance, so far away that it seemed like an illusion. He listened. There was no sound except the muffled murmur behind the darkness, and the sound of footsteps behind him, approaching slowly.

---

1. The *tar* is a traditional Iranian string instrument.
2. *Sofre-ye nazr:* a votive ceremony, during which food is blessed and distributed among the guests.

3

Mr. Azizi sat down, stretched out his legs, and leaned his head back. He folded his hands, and said to himself: "If only I'd just go. If only I'd get up. If only I weren't here. How many thousand times do I have to eat Mr. Heydari's birthday cake? I don't have any more room for it. I never did. From the first day I didn't want to eat it, but I ate it. I laughed. I nodded my head and said, 'Mmmm, it's delicious!' Why? Was it that I didn't want to hurt his feelings? Or maybe because all our friends insisted? I don't know. All I could see was that I was eating, more and more, faster and faster. I wanted to throw up, but I just kept on munching away, taking bigger and bigger bites. I finished off the crumbs on the plate and licked my fingers. I ate from my wife's plate and from the plate next to me. I wanted to say no, to say I don't want any, I don't like it. But I was too embarrassed. I wanted to smash my plate against the wall, but instead I clung to it so it wouldn't drop. I even got another plateful, held it right up to my chin and kept on eating. But I can't do it anymore. I'm stuffed with birthday cake; my head, my ears, my hair, my dreams are full of all the friends' birthday cakes: Mr. Heydari, Anvari, Hashemi and all the rest

21

of them. So the best thing is for me to leave, right this minute: one, two, three."

He looked for his arms, his legs, his tired body that had slumped down into the sofa, his scattered thoughts. He knew he existed, since it was Heydari's birthday, since he could hear his watch ticking, since someone had just said: "I'm pleased to meet you, sir," since his friends had just drunk to his new job, since his card was pinned to the flowers he had brought and he could see it shining from across the room, since his wife was pregnant again, since he could see his reflection moving in the full-length mirror on the wall, and since someone was complimenting him on his cufflinks and on the fine material his trousers were made of. Nonetheless, he still couldn't find himself. His limbs were disconnected, and his body had no contour. It was as if he were an extension of the man standing next to him or of the woman looking at him from across the room.

Someone said something to him and slapped him on the shoulder. "Isn't that so!" the man said.

His wife whispered into his ear: "Dear, be careful what you say; it's full of strangers here."

Azizi nodded and cautiously eyed the man standing next to him. He took a bite of the cucumber he was holding and forced himself to chew it.

Across from him, on the wall, was a full-length mirror. In it was half of his head, half of his face, and half of his shoulder. He looked at himself, at his mouth that was full and his teeth with green pieces of cucumber stuck between them, at his round head and his red ears that hung next to his hair like wrinkled balls of fat. "Is that me?" he wondered.

He straightened up to see himself better. His neck was lost between his fleshy shoulders, and his skin had a yellowish hue from the rolls of fat beneath it. He had come to look like an air mattress, soft, puffed up and ample. He couldn't believe it. He turned away and said to himself: "Those aren't my eyes, that isn't me looking, those aren't my arms and legs, that isn't my body."

22

He thought of himself, of the image he had of a person named Azizollah Azizi. He pictured himself among his friends: taller than all of them, nimbler, healthier, happier. He pictured himself throughout all the days and the moments, here and there, impatient and passionate—and always waiting, waiting for life, waiting for the days to come, for something bigger and better than what he had, than what there was.

He'd said: "Friends, so much for education and degrees. I'm through; that's over. Now it's time for life. Move over, it's my turn!"

He saw himself as he was when he first fell in love: dizzy, star-struck, blissful. He swore and made promises, to himself and to that pale, plumpish girl. He had planned his life in meticulous detail, and laughed at all the suspicious and unbelieving looks. "Friends," he'd said, "God is on my side. This is the girl I've been looking for."

He remembered the day they shaved his head; his soldier's uniform didn't fit, the trousers were too tight and too short. Hashemi had brought him a pot of food; it was a bad night. His friends had lined up along the bus. Anvari was holding his suitcase. It was snowing, and someone behind him was weeping. The faces, from behind the steamed-up window, didn't look human. He had tried to keep his friends from hearing his voice. "Two years of military service is no big deal, my dearest," he had said. "It will be over in no time. I'm not going off to die!"

He tried to remember that round face with the thin, pale lips and the chubby legs, that forgotten creature who had been the sole object of all his meticulous planning. His first night as a soldier, he hadn't been able to sleep. The next night his body had hurt all over. The nights afterward he had been cold, and his mind had frozen over just thinking of the cold. Nonetheless, he had counted the days to himself. He had crossed off each month and had waited for those two years to end. They had come to an end, but so had many other things.

"What are you thinking about, dear?" his wife asked. Azizi raised his head and uttered a quick laugh. He remembered

23

that he mustn't do anything unusual, like remembering too much, seeing too much, thinking too much, or being happy or unhappy too much. He must only be, as succinctly as possible, among all the hands and voices and feet, among all the chairs and plates and windows, among the forks and the spoons.

Mr. Heydari was watching him from afar.

Mr. Azizi turned to the stranger standing next to him and said: "Wouldn't you care to sit down? " and moved over to make room. He listened to the voice whispering in his ear, and looked into the face across from his. He raised his glass of wine to Mr. Heydari's health and drank.

He said to himself: "I wish that damned mirror weren't there on the wall." He turned away from it and looked around him, at the striped, fringed curtains, at the flowered wallpaper, at the color photographs of Mr. Heydari on the walls, at the mirror frame, the tables, the bowls and dishes displayed on the buffet, at the crystal vases on the tables, at the silver candelabra covered with plastic. He looked at the artificial flowers, at the porcelain figurines, at the glass dog, cat and birds over the heater, at the lampshades with dangling pompoms, at the radio and television sets under their slipcovers, at the leopard skin on the carpet and the moose head over the door, at the wind-up doll that chimed and had a light flashing on and off under her skirt, at the extra tables and metal chairs, at the odd boxes and empty bottles.

He was scared. His gaze was lost among all these things. He didn't know how it would be possible to get past all of them, over to the other side of the room. It would take a lifetime, an eternity. He wished he were anywhere but here. He wished he would get up and leave.

"Well," he'd said, "so much for military service. It's been two bad years, but they passed. Now it's time for life!" Of course, the idea of living without that pale, plumpish girl didn't appeal to him much; but as his friends had said, these things happen. He saw her once again, from afar, with her husband and child. And then he didn't think about her anymore.

"What are you looking at, dear? " his wife asked. Azizi sat up straight, stifled a sneeze, took out his handkerchief and carefully wiped off the corners of his mouth. He shook the crumbs off his trousers and smiled at the other guests.

One of them, standing across the room, looked happy. He was talking to everyone and asking them how they were.

Another, far away, was describing his strange stomach aches and dizzy spells. He knew the names of all the doctors and was cursing all of them.

Another was trying to solve some unknown equation. He was talking to himself and writing numbers in the air, multiplying and dividing.

Another was talking about himself, and looking out of the corner of his eye at his reflection in the full-length mirror on the wall.

Another was riveted to his half-finished crossword puzzle. He had chewed up his pencil; he'd even chewed away the corners of the newspaper. He'd pulled the buttons off his jacket, and the skin around his nails was bleeding.

Another wasn't doing anything.

Azizi stole a glance at his watch, and remembered that if he wanted to go, he'd better get moving before it was too late.

There was a knock at the door. From the hall came the sound of greetings and kisses, the rustle of silk skirts and the squeak of new shoes.

Someone asked: "Well, when are they going to bring out Heydari's birthday cake?"

Azizi looked at the door, at the window, at the hole in the wall for the stovepipe. He tried to pull himself together and get on his feet. He couldn't. It was as if a thousand steel weights had been tied to his body, and the pull of gravity was increasing by the moment. His shirt collar was too tight and his new shoes were hurting his feet. He wanted to take off his tie, to break the belt buckle that had burrowed into his stomach and throw it away. He felt like taking his glasses, his watch, his turquoise and agate rings, his necktie pins, his heavy stone cufflinks, his metal cigarette case and his silver lighter, his gold fountain pens, his keys to the house, the car and the closets, his appointment book and his calendar. . . he felt like taking them all off and throwing them away, so that he might feel lighter, breathe, get up and go.

From outside came the sound of the wind blowing, of feet moving, of night passing through the city. Outside the window there were things happening. There was space, and sky, and streets to walk away on. Beyond those walls was the world, life, history, and a thousand new and wonderful moments; out there one could stand and watch and inquire and perhaps find something new; from out there one could begin anew and be, and then go beyond all these things and reach another peak, then move on again and be again.

"Make conversation, dear. " his wife said. "Be your usual self!"

The man working on the crossword puzzle whispered into his ear: "It only has three letters. The first one is 'A' and the last one is 'Q. ' 'Atq'? 'Ajq'? 'Asq'?[1] What is it? "

"Forgive me. " said Azizi. "I don't know. I'm very sorry." Anvari wanted to read him Mahdavi's letter. It was twenty pages long. Azizi tried to look interested and be patient. He said to himself: "What should I do? Should I leave or wait till he's finished? What if I hurt his feelings? What if he gets upset?"

"Heydari-jan," he had said, "I appreciate your kindness. But this job isn't for me. I can't be an office worker. I can't stay put in one room, or stay in the same place. You know me."

Anvari had said: "You old fool, this is a kind of experience too. A man can't just hang around with nothing to do."

Hashemi had said: "It wouldn't be nice to break Heydari's heart. Take the job for a while, and then if you don't like it, quit."

"Alright," he'd said, "just for you. And just for a few months. Maybe even just for a few days."

Anvari's voice was spinning in his head: Mahdavi had fallen into the pool; he'd been drowning. Talat had come and pulled him out. She had struggled to help him catch his breath and

26

then she had beaten on him until finally he'd started breathing again.

Heydari said: "Amazing! God has truly shown mercy."

Anvari said: "But their new neighbor is even more amazing! Right now he's a dentist; before he was a tailor, and once he was even a singer on the radio. He's pulled four of Mahdavi's teeth. He's pulled the mayor's teeth and his deputy's teeth. He's pulled half the city's teeth! Except for Talat-khanom. She punched him and knocked him right over."

Several people said: "That's really amazing!"

Hashemi sat himself down with difficulty on the sofa next to Azizi. He put his arm around Azizi's shoulder. He picked up the photo album on the table and leafed through it, sighing.

Shirin-khanom was standing in a corner, feeling out of sorts. She was still in black, and her sorrow over Ahmadi had made her ill. Her gaze was familiar: it was drawing something from the depth of Azizi's heart, something long gone and forgotten.

Hashemi poked him in the ribs with his elbow. "Did you see this picture? It's from June 1948. Dear old Heydari's birthday. We're all there, arm in arm, just like always."

Azizi thought back to that night and cringed. He thought back to June of 1949 and June of 1950 and '51 and '52. He looked at Heydari and Anvari, at Hashemi and Asgari. He thought of June of 1978 and June of 1988 and June of 2008 and June of 2018. He pictured Heydari's two-thousandth birthday and shuddered, muttering to himself: "We're all there, faithful skeletons, arm in arm, just like tonight. All together, with an album three thousand pages long with one million snapshots. With a big cake and two thousand candles; and then again the year after, and the year after that, forever."

All the Friends had said: "Congratulations, 'Boss'! That's an impressive title!" He'd answered: "What? You must be joking! Don't tell me you really think I care about that kind of thing! Have you forgotten what I said? "

They had sent for a photographer too.

Someone had said: "Let's take a picture to commemorate the occasion of Mr. Heydari's fortieth birthday."

Azizi looked at the photographer sadly. His wife came and stood behind him. She bent over and put her hands around his neck, saying: "Hold your head up."

Azizi raised his head and said to himself: "June of 2008 is there, waiting for me, looking at me. All the moments of my past and future are there, riveted, fixed; just one picture, one eternal picture."

Hashemi said: "Wait, let my little Shirin come too. " Azizi took his hand off the arm of the sofa so that Shirin could sit down.

"Look into the camera," his wife said.

Azizi looked. Hashemi's head was under his chin, Shirin's head on his shoulder.

"Sit closer." said the photographer.

Someone was passing out plates of cake to everyone.

Azizi thought: "Nobody has the right to tell me not to go when I want to go. Nobody has the right to tell me to shut up when I want to talk. When I want to live, nobody can tell me to drop dead, and drop dead quietly. Nobody can pin me to a spot as if I were a dried-up insect. If anything is going to happen, it's going to happen outside this room. There's only shadows and darkness here, with the precise calculation of birthdays—the thirtieth, the fortieth, the sixtieth—people marking time with precision, counting things, panicking about nothingness, and talk, talk, talk. No. I can't sit and watch it anymore. I must get up, right now. All I have to do is get my arm out from behind Hashemi's back, take my wife's hand off my neck, lift Shirin-khanom's head off my shoulder, remove the bowl of dried fruit and nuts from my lap, pull my legs out from under the table, and go!'

"Dear," his wife said, "when they bring out Mr. Heydari's birthday cake, I want you to get up and sing. "

Jalili had said: "If a person wants to go, he doesn't ask, he doesn't wait. He goes. "

He'd said:"Jalili-jan, I know. You're right. But I'm tired. I can't get up. I've worked all day. I was awake all night. I feel heavy. My head's spinning. I have a stomach ache. Why don't you understand? "

Shirin-khanom had said: "Oh, Mr. Azizi! Why have you grown so fat? It's scary!"

There was the sound of applause and cheers, and the clinking of forks and spoons.

They had brought out Heydari's birthday cake. It was covered with little red and yellow candles. Azizi shuddered. His wife asked: "Are you ready?" Hashemi was all excited; he was clapping and jumping up and down. Anvari said: "Now's the time! Come on!"

Azizi said to himself: "No, this won't do. They're looking at me. I have to figure out a way to leave without anybody noticing. The best way is for me to go into the bathroom and lock the door. When they're busy with something else, I climb out of the bathroom window and jump into the empty courtyard. I go into the kitchen and out the back door into the greenhouse. Then I listen. No sound. I crawl among the flowerpots on my hands and knees. I climb over the bower and onto the wall. I climb onto the streetlamp post; I slide down. I'm in the street. I look around. No one's watching me. I start running; I take a right; keep running; I take a left. I run farther and farther away. What new strength I've found! What speed! My body has shed all its fleshy overweight and the earth has lost its gravity. I keep going, going; I soar! It's as if I've emerged from the earth's atmosphere; I'm floating. No one and nothing can reach me, even wind, even light!"

A voice next to his ear said: "Go over there, in the middle, in front of everyone."

Azizi looked at the faces next to his. Anvari said: "Sing loud and clear."

Hashemi grabbed him under the arms and lifted him onto his feet.

Asgari laughed: "Were you asleep? "

Shirin-khanom said: "Leave him alone. He doesn't want to sing."

They made way for him. The photographer said: "Sir, allow me to take a picture of just you."

Someone asked: "What does he want to sing? " Someone pushed him from behind.

His wife said: "Everyone be quiet. My husband is about to sing."

Azizi took a breath with difficulty.

They were all waiting, laughing. They had made a circle around him, and were banging their forks against their plates.

Someone said: "Move aside, please."

Someone tugged at his sleeve. Another took him by the arm.

Azizi's eyes searched for the door. He was surrounded with arms, eyes and mouths. He realized he was in the middle of the room, that he was whirling around himself.

Someone was flipping the lights on and off. Voices were chanting in unison: "Azizi must sing! Azizi must sing!"

Azizi thought of the person out there in the street, who had grown wings, who was somewhere else, who was gone.

"Hurry up!" his wife said. "You've kept everyone waiting."

Someone said: "Sir, we are waiting for your song."

Azizi felt dizzy, and his heart felt heavier than ever. He wanted to scream. He wanted to smash everything to pieces. He said to himself: "What song? What do I care that it's Heydari's birthday? If he's so happy, let him sing. Isn't he the one who's successful and happy? Isn't he the winner and the conqueror? So why is he hunched over in a corner, not saying anything? What's the matter with him? Why is he so pale? Look at him stare at the candles on his cake. Forty years of his life are there, mixed with all the cream and the egg yolks. What should I sing for him? A song of love, a song of freedom, or a song of death? "

Heydari's birthday cake was in everyone's mouths.

Someone said: "Clap, everybody!"

Anvari was drumming the beat on the back of a tray. Azizi said to himself: "All I have to do is open my mouth and scream."

His wife said: "Louder! Livelier!"

Hashemi said: "Come on, let's all lock arms. Let's all sing

together."

All of them began to sing, with one voice, from the bottom of their hearts.

Azizi strained his throat.

"What's wrong with you? " said his wife. "Why are you standing with your mouth open? "

The Friends were dancing. The Friends were drunk. Hashemi had balanced his glass on his forehead and was shimmying his shoulders. Several people, sitting cross-legged among the arms and the legs, over in the corner, were playing cards hurriedly. Someone was sick and throwing up in the bathroom.

Someone said: "Are you all right, sir? "

Azizi just looked at him.

Anvari said: "Clap, everybody! Clap! Clap!"

Shirin-khanom said: "Would you like to go outside and take a walk with me? "

Azizi just looked at her.

Hashemi said: "Come on, pal. Get up and dance! Dance!"

His wife said: "You'd better sit down, dear. "

Azizi saw that he was back in his place. The back of the sofa felt soft and familiar under his neck. He stretched his legs under the table and kicked off his shoes. He wiggled his toes and rubbed his aching corn against the table leg. The arms of the sofa awaited his arms, and Heydari's birthday cake tasted the same as always in his mouth.

---

1. These combinations are also meaningless in Persian.

4

What a faint lamp. It lights only itself and the bugs hovering around it. I'm cold, as if this snow that has been falling so hard all night has settled on my heart. These hands still need to get warm, these old, decrepit hands.

It's exactly nine o'clock.

Today has come to an end. Thank God. It wasn't a good day. It was long and cold and dark. And nothing happened. I have to wait till summer comes. The sunshine will make me warm again; at least my legs won't ache so much. Six months isn't long. I'll wait. If anything is going to happen, it's going to happen in the summer. I'm sure.

I get up. I have dinner by the wall next to the heater. A plate, a glass, a spoon, a bowl of yogurt, a pot of rice left over from lunchtime. I set them all out. It's still early. At nine I warm up the rice on the heater. At ten past nine I eat dinner. At ten I get under the covers and wait to fall asleep.

I pour a little yogurt into a glass and sip it. It's tasty; I leave half for later.

Azizi said: "What 'later'? "

"To hell with later. " said Jalili. "If you have something to say, say it now."

Anvari said: "One should persevere. One should laugh, go forward and say to oneself 'How happy I am!'"

But even he didn't believe it anymore. He no longer laughed or spoke about being happy. Maybe if Mahdavi hadn't gone away with Talat-khanom things would have been different. Maybe if that uninvited guest hadn't come onto the scene he would have really believed in happiness.

"Mahdavi-jan," I said, "what about Anvari? Without you he'll die of grief. You two grew up together; you were as one person. No one's ever seen one of you without the other. And now you're just going to up and go? How could you? Don't do it. Take him with you. Convince your wife to let him go with you."

Talat-khanom was standing in the courtyard. Her head reached the top of the doorway. She looked like the tree at Emamzadeh Qassem, frightful, imposing and ancient. The wind was blowing her hair this way and that. Her body gave off a kind of animal heat. Her skin smelled like sheep, like fresh milk and dung, like village garden paths.

"Talat-khanom," I said, "let me help you. You can't carry this by yourself." She threw my hand aside and stepped on my foot. She had put Anvari's carpet into the courtyard. She had put the sofa and chairs around the fountain pool, saying: "From now on, everything in this house belongs to Mahdavi. It's mine."

Mahdavi was sitting on a chair next to the fountain pool, pale and sad, stunned and resigned. His hands lay on his lap and his head drooped. His lower lip quivered. Talat-khanom was keeping an eye on him; she'd made him some lemonade; she caressed him gently, waving the flies away from his face.

"Talat-khanom," I said, "let Anvari go along with you." She had bent down to tie Mahdavi's shoelace. She didn't answer.

Anvari couldn't believe it. He was sitting in the middle of the room and was staring at Mahdavi's suitcase. He said nothing. He had no energy. He didn't even breathe. He was like someone who had been put to sleep.

"Anvari-jan," I said, "don't think about it. It isn't the end of the world."

He looked up at me, and said: "The monster came and took my friend away. And took him so easily!"

But why am I thinking of these things anyway? Now that I must sleep. Now that I must forget. Now that it's too late, for everything.

Azizi said: "What if we still have memories after we die? What if under all that earth we wake up and remember everything?"

I look at the picture of Heydari on the wall. He's standing among all the friends, one step in front of everyone. Out of the corner of his eye he looks at the candles on his birthday cake. Shirin-khanom has her head bent, and her little finger is in her mouth. Azizi is there too, in the corner of the picture; only half of his face can be seen; maybe there's some dirt over it, or maybe the sun has faded it; I don't know, it's an old picture.

Two fat rats are peeking out from the middle of the sofa. There are several others; more come out at night. They've gnawed away at everything, the furniture, the hem on the curtains, the corners of the sheet, the rims of my shoes. I bang on their heads with my spoon. They just look at me. They're not afraid of anything anymore, not even of a spoon banged on their heads or a shoe flung at them.

I feel like going out for a walk, even if it's snowing, even it it's deadly cold. Back in the old days we had a house and a little garden. We were neighbors with Anvari.

We would sleep on the roof and talk to each other from one roof to another. He was waiting for Mahdavi. Every night he would lay out bedding for him and place a glass of icewater next to it. He'd say: "He'll be coming back. I'm sure of it. One of these very days he's going to show up."

We went to the train station. He'd written to say he was coming. "See! Didn't I tell you!" said Anvari. He'd stayed awake all night. He would call to me and then forget what he wanted. He'd gotten up at the crack of dawn and was hosing down the courtyard. He'd put flowers in the vases, and

34

couldn't take his eyes off his watch.

"What's the matter with you?" said Heydari. "Wait till the train comes to a stop; you're going to fall under it. Stand aside."

"Wait for the doors to open." said Azizi.

Anvari giggled and held the bouquet of flowers he'd brought for Mahdavi before his face. His eyes twinkled. "He's going to step out of that door, isn't he?" he asked.

Our eyes fell upon Talat-khanom, on her tousled red hair and the men's shoes she always wore.

"I came instead of him." she said. "He doesn't have what it takes to deal with you guys."

She jumped off and grabbed Heydari by the collar. She demanded her husband's money back. We tried to stop her, but it was no use. She pushed us away and shouted. She punched Heydari in the stomach and twisted his arm.

Anvari, with his bouquet, was standing behind the newspaper stand, peeking out warily. He trembled. "Oh my God," he said, "now she's going to come after me." That night I kept an eye on him from my roof. Talat-khanom slept in Mahdavi's bedding. Her feet stuck out over the edge of the mattress. She was hot; she tossed and turned, she scratched herself. Anvari was sitting over by the steps of the roof. With every snore Talat-khanom made he would jump up and run.

"Heydari-jan," I said, "maybe you'd better give her back her husband's money so she'll go."

"It's my fault'" he said, "for worrying so much about your future, all of you. I've put all of your money in the bank: in two years it will have doubled, in ten years it will have tripled, in twenty years it will have quadrupled. In a hundred years it will be worth ten times as much! The account number is 631. Just think, it's constantly progressing!"

"That man's a bastard." said Talat-khanom. "He's swindled all of you. Don't listen to him."

We were at Anvari's house. Who was there? It was the summer after, or the last summer. I don't remember. We were sitting around his bed. He'd been sick for two months, and nothing we did helped. Hashemi had brought one of his homemade brews. "Drink this," he said, "you'll get well. It'll take away your fever."

Heydari suggested: "Why don't we contact Mahdavi? It's being so heartsick over Mahdavi that's gotten him into this mess."

"Let's take him to Gorgan." said Azizi.

Anvari's head was resting against my arm. I was holding his neck and pouring the brew that Hashemi had brought into his mouth, one spoonful at a time.

I happened to look at Heydari. I saw that he was pale, and his mouth was hanging open. I turned around and looked. Talat-khanom, covered with dust, her old cardboard suitcase in her hand, was standing in the doorway. She was tired and out of breath.

Anvari raised his head and threw up the brew. He lept to the far corner of the bed and clung to the sheets. "I knew it!" he said. "It's her. She's come to kill me!"

Hashemi said: "Talat-khanom, leave him alone. We're taking care of him."

"We've brought a doctor over." said Azizi. "There's nothing wrong with him."

"Don't leave me alone with her!" Anvari begged. "Don't listen to her!"

He held the sheets close, and his lower lip quivered. He had sat up half way and was hurriedly looking for his shoes. "Don't leave," he said, "for God's sake don't leave!"

We tried to stay. We tried not to leave. It was no use. Talat-khanom threw us out and shut the door in our faces. We returned in the evening and peeked through the window blinds.

Azizi said: "What's that pot of boiling water for?"

Heydari said: "She's come to eat him."

Anvari was quietly weeping. He couldn't take his eyes off the pot of hot water. He was muttering to himself and crawling around in his bed on all fours. His face was covered with the steam from the pot.

Azizi said: "We ought to go in and stop this."

Talat-khanom wanted some towels. We handed her some through the door and ran back to our places by the window.

Heydari said: "She's not going to leave until she's taken the life out of him."

"Talat-khanom," I said, "let me come in." She didn't answer. She was busy.

She had taken off her blouse. Her red brassiere was dripping with sweat. Her armpits were covered with black, curly hair. She was panting like a tired horse, and thick plumes of vapor streamed out of her nostrils.

"She's stripping him." said Azizi.

"I wish we'd called a policeman. " said Heydari.

Anvari was clinging to the cuff of his trousers and screaming.

We settled down to watch. Talat-khanom would take the towels out of the hot water, wring them out and lay them over Anvari. Anvari was squirming and calling out Mahdavi's name. Once he even got up and tried to run away. He made it to the door; Talat-khanom grabbed him by the waist and tossed him back into bed.

"What's that she's pouring down his throat? " asked Hashemi.

"Deadly poison." said Heydari.

"She's killing him." said Azizi.

"I'm going to file a complaint." said Heydari. "I'm going to report all of this."

Anvari had gradually given in. He lay face down on the bed and made no sound.

Talat-khanom gathered up the towels and placed the pot by the wall. She then rolled Anvari tightly between two blankets and tucked him under the quilt. She tied a scarf around his head, then sat next to his bed and waited for him to fall asleep.

We came back early the next morning. Azizi said: "Talat-khanom, get up and go get some sleep." She was sitting at Anvari's bedside, wiping the perspiration from his face. She had deep circles under her eyes. "Just hand me a cigarette. "

she said.

We returned the next evening. She wouldn't let us in. We left her tray of food at the door and left. "Anvari's dead." said Heydari. "I'm sure of it."

We returned the evening after. "What is it? " she said. "What's the matter with you? Why do you keep coming here every day? "

Heydari said: "It smells like a corpse."

We waited for a week, then ran out of patience.

Heydari said: "I dropped by there yesterday. There was a pile of dirt in the middle of the garden. She's buried him there." We waited one more day, and then went all together. The door to his room was open. Anvari was sitting in the middle of his bed, slowly sipping tea. He still had the scarf on his head. His fever had gone.

Hashemi said: "You must be tired, Talat-khanom; don't leave so soon."

Azizi said: "Stay and get some rest."

She had put her suitcase by the door. When she saw Heydari her eyes glared. She jumped up and said: "Hold it, you bastard. I have some business to settle with you!"

She was a good woman, the "colonel." I look at her wedding picture still on the wall; it's dusty and blurred. Anvari and Mahdavi and Hashemi and I are standing next to her. The lights on her head are out.

She was a good woman. I'd like to go and visit her. I'd like to write her a letter and ask her how she is. My heart still yearns for so many things, things that are now lost.

Azizi said: "I wish at least we still had our eyes, and we could sit and watch—watch life."

I get up. I turn up the flame in the heater. I put the pot of rice on top. I light the wick in the cookstove. The handle on my frying pan is broken. One of these days I'm going to go out and buy some new things. I put the frying pan on the cookstove and crack two eggs into it. I sit and wait. Tomorrow night I'll invite the landlord over for dinner. Or I'll drop in on the neighbors. Or I'll just sit here and count the rats. Last night there were eleven of them. I caught one and threw it into the heater. Tonight I'll play another game, one that's more fun. As Heydari used to say: "One should always keep oneself busy. One should laugh and say, 'How very happy I am!'"

5

Anvari carefully placed the suitcase above his head; he waved to Hashemi, Heydari, Azizi, and Shirin-khanom, who were standing outside the train window, and thanked them for everything. He showed Heydari the keys to his suitcase which were pinned to his lapel, and signaled to him that there was nothing to worry about. He put the bird that Shirin-khanom had given him to take to Mr. Mahdavi on the floor next to his seat. He looked at the other passengers and smiled, then asked: "How come the train isn't leaving?"

No one answered him.

He sat down and put the potted geranium Hashemi had brought him on his lap. He blinked incredulously, took a deep breath and said to himself: "I've finally left. I'm really going."

He still remembered that last day. Mahdavi had poked his head out the car window and said: "You come too. Take the first train out tonight. " Mahdavi didn't want to leave. He wouldn't get into the car. Talat-khanom had grabbed him by the collar and dragged him in.

The Friends had said: "Anvari-jan, it isn't as if Gorgan is at the other end of the world. You can go visit him any time you like." Anvari had looked away. His head had drooped and his friends had seen that his chin was quivering. He'd gone into the house, slammed the door, and they could hear him kicking the walls. He had shattered the flower pots, pulled all the ivy out by the roots, and wept.

Anvari had said: "I can't stay in this house without my Mahdavi-jan any longer. I'm leaving tomorrow for Gorgan."

But he hadn't left. He didn't leave two days later either, or a week later or a month later or even a year later. What did it matter, seven days or seven years? As long as he was finally going.

Heydari was tapping on the window. He was saying something that he didn't want the other people in Anvari's compartment to hear.

Anvari put the flower pot down next to the bird and got up. He grabbed the handle on the window and pulled; it wouldn't open. He pulled harder; it still wouldn't open. He pulled with both hands, but still it was no use.

The other passengers were looking at him. "How do you open this? " he asked.

The man sitting next to the window answered: "It doesn't open at all.

"It doesn't? " said Anvari, and he signaled to Heydari that the window didn't open.

He sat down, and asked: "What's wrong? Has something happened? Why aren't we leaving? "

The woman sitting next to him said: "Mister, that bird and that flowerpot are in the way. You can't leave them like that."

Anvari said: "Yes, of course!" and hurriedly picked up the bird and the flowerpot and held them both in his arms. He looked at the other passengers and smiled. He was happy to be sitting next to the window, happy to be able to look at everything, to count the trees and read the names on the shops and street signs. He wanted to introduce himself and ask the other passengers their names. He wanted to tell them how happy he was, how excited and giddy. He wanted to talk, about the beautiful weather, about the expansion of the public transportation system, about the man who'd killed his wife with a butcher's cleaver, about the big prizes given out by the Everlasting Jewel Company, about the price of land plots in Aliabad, about his weird dreams and the strange pains in his stomach, about his dark and lonely nights, about how much he missed Mahdavi, about his fears and anxieties, about himself. There were other things he wanted to talk about too. But the woman next to him was scowling and her knitting needles were frightfully sharp. Her daughter was sitting next to her, carefully blowing into a large balloon that had grown as taut and thin as an onion skin.

Anvari said to her: "That's enough, dear; it's going to burst."

The woman looked at him from the corner of her eye. She unraveled what she had knitted and started over again. Anvari leaned over and stifled a sneeze. Shirin-khanom's bird was chirping and pecking at the polka-dots on his tie.

The man reading the newspaper looked over the corner of the page with one eye and stared at Anvari.

Anvari looked with horror at the black eye staring at him, and hastily said: "Hello! How do you do? "

The balloon burst.

Anvari jumped, caught the flowerpot upside down in mid-air, grabbed the bird that was frantically flapping its wings, and looked at the girl indignantly.

"So what's the matter?" said the woman. "It's her balloon."

Anvari regained his composure. He smiled, nodded and stared at his shoes.

The man sitting next to the door said: "Nope. There's no way we're going to leave today."

"So what. " said the woman. "Things can't get any worse." It was twenty minutes past departure time.

Heydari had said: "It's an unnecessary trip. What a waste of time and money."

Shirin-khanom had said: "Go. Go for sure. Don't worry about anything."

Hashemi had said: "Whatever God wills."

The whistle sounded, and the train started off. Anvari raised his head and asked: "Are we moving? "

"God knows. " answered the woman.

Anvari beat against the window and waved to his friends. He hugged Shirin-khanom's bird and looked kindly at the girl, who was now blowing into another balloon. His latest picture of Mahdavi and Talat-khanom was in his pocket. He took it out and looked at it. Mahdavi had grown heavier, balder, older. He didn't look like himself. He looked as if his teeth had fallen out. Also, his nose was broader and his neck shorter. His voice on the telephone was different, unfamiliar. Even his handwriting had changed; it was smaller and hard to read. But in spite of all this, he was still himself, the same old Mr. Mahdavi. Anvari had three albums of pictures of Mahdavi. Pictures from his childhood, pictures from his youth, and wedding pictures. In all the childhood pictures they were together, two fat little shrimps with bare bottoms and curly hair. They were hand in hand, an arm on each other's shoulder. They'd flunked sixth grade and eighth grade together, they'd both had a C-average in seventh grade, and had earned zeros in gym. In the later pictures, of their youth, they were also together, with skimpy moustaches and crooked parts and slicked-down hair, wearing laced-up shoes and checkered suits.

Heydari would always say: "Those two have been together for so long, they've grown to look alike. They talk alike, walk alike, laugh alike. They get sick together; they get well together. Two nice faithful lambs. May God keep them!"

He had another picture too, and he took it out and looked at it. Talat-khanom hadn't changed at all—same shaggy red hair, same intrepid black eyes, same long neck and white teeth.

They'd nicknamed her "the colonel" and they knew that she beat Mahdavi. Once she'd bashed in the head of the neighborhood policeman. And once she'd even kicked the daylights out of Heydari. In spite of all that, Heydari would always say: "That woman is valuable. She's useful. She's a shield against disaster. Whatever our Mahdavi has, he owes it to her, his house, his job, his social standing, his respectablity, his silver tea-glass holders. " She would sit on the porch and tweeze the hair on her legs; she'd put quince and orange peels on her windowsill so her room would smell nice. She drove a jeep and shouted curses at everyone. She drank. She sang and danced. She'd shimmy her breasts and raise her skirt. She'd cry, too, whenever she saw a child or a pregnant woman, or when she'd listen to Zan-Agha, the cleaning lady, or to Ali, the lottery-ticket seller.

The compartment door opened. The ticket inspector looked in and counted the passengers.

Anvari hurriedly asked: "When will we get there? "

The ticket inspector shrugged his shoulders and looked at the passengers. "What's that? " he asked.

"It's a bird. " said Anvari. "Look, it's completely ruined my trousers."

The inspector said: "All of you step out of the compartment."

Anvari looked at the other passengers terrified and asked: "What's happened? "

"Come on, move it!" said the inspector.

Anvari picked up the bird and the flowerpot and followed the others out.

There was no one else in the corridor. From the next compartment came the sound of people arguing, of a speech on the radio and of a child crying.

The inspector knelt down and looked under the seats. He'd emptied the handbags onto the floor.

Anvari said: "That's my suitcase!" and quickly opened the door of the compartment.

"What do you want? " said the inspector.

The passengers were standing around them. They watched. Anvari put the bird and the flowerpot down and knelt to unlock his suitcase. The inspector put his hand inside the suitcase, under the clothes, and slowly slid it forward. He stopped, and looked up. He looked Anvari right in the eye and asked: "What's this? "

44

The other passengers drew closer and tightened the circle. Their heads were bent over the suitcase.

"That's a batch of letters. They're from one of my friends, Mr. Mahdavi."

The inspector ripped off the string around the letters. The woman said: "What have *we* done wrong? How long do *we* have to stand and wait? "

The man next to the door looked suspiciously at Anvari and whispered something to the person next to him. Anvari wiped his face with his hand, which had inexplicably gone cold and limp, and tried to breathe calmly. His heart was heavy and was beating erratically.

The man next to the door said:"And what's that?"

"It's a kind of accordion," said Anvari. "It's a toy. It belongs to him too."

"What's that? " said the woman.

"These are albums. Photo albums. See, this is Mr. Mahdavi, this is Talat-khanom. That's me, I'm barely four years old; they've shaved my head."

"I have to take these letters." said the inspector.

"What for? " said Anvari.

"Why do you argue, mister?" said the woman.

Anvari reached out and grabbed the edge of the batch of letters. The ticket inspector turned around and looked at him.

Anvari let his hand drop and put it in his pocket. He took it back out and sadly scratched his head.

"When will you give them back? " he asked. "Later," said the inspector as he left.

The passengers sat down again. The woman gathered her things together and put them back into her purse, muttering curses.

Anvari locked his suitcase and put it back. He tightened his belt. He buttoned his fly, which was open, and looked at the other passengers. He felt a dull, burning pain at the top of his stomach, but he didn't show it. He sat down and stretched out his legs. He was hot, and the sound of the train's wheels ground inside his head. His stomach grumbled with each jolt, and he was feeling emptier and emptier. The bottom of the flowerpot was damp, and he could't figure out how to hold it without getting a stain on his trousers. Shirin-khanom's bird wouldn't calm down, and kept pecking at everything.

The girl showed Anvari her balloon, which was about to burst, and slowly blew into it.

Anvari felt he was getting angry, but he controlled himself and tried to be happy. He said to himself: "Tonight we'll be together. I'm almost there. " He thought the best thing to do would be to whistle. He puckered his lips and stared at a point. But he didn't know how. He'd never learned. Time after time he'd practiced with Hashemi and Heydari, but to no avail. Shirin-khanom whistled better than all of them: she knew all the different ways. She would sit next to the window and whistle, imitating birds—nightingales, canaries, swallows, and birds no one had ever heard, sounds no one had ever heard. Heydari knew how to whistle too. His whistling was loud and precise and serious. Anvari only knew how to pucker his lips, stare at a point, flare his nostrils and push the air out through his lips. But even that wasn't bad; it was something.

The other passengers were looking at him.

Anvari laughed and said: "I'm whistling. That's something. It makes a person feel light-hearted."

The woman irritatedly knitted a few rows, and then asked: "Is that stinking smell coming from you? "

Mr. Anvari hung his head and looked down at his shiny shoes. "No, it isn't." he said. "It's coming from the bird here. This bird has soiled itself, and it has also completely ruined my trousers. "

The woman's skein of yarn had rolled off her lap and disappeared under the seat.

The man next to the door muttered something and shook his head. Mr. Anvari asked: "Excuse me, were you talking to me?"

The woman was looking around her. "Allow me. " said Mr. Anvari. "I'll get it for you." and he put the bird and the flowerpot down, stooped over and retrieved the yarn from under the seat.

The man next to the window said: "God help us."

Anvari fixed his tie, which was loose, and shook the knees of his trousers. "I won't get up again." he said to himself. "They're right; with so little room, one shouldn't move around."

He closed his eyes and thought of six hours later. Shirin-khanom had said: "But Mr. Anvari, what are you afraid of? Huh? " He'd thought about this trip for seven years. And Mahdavi was waiting for him. His voice on the phone was trembling. He'd written him twenty-seven letters, and he still didn't believe it. The picture showed that deep in his eyes were sorrow and shame.

Heydari had laughed. "Mahdavi is just like a lamb," he'd said, "a sacred lamb. You'd want to sacrifice him. You'd want to cook him with rice and eat him up."

Anvari didn't notice when he'd fallen asleep. When he opened his eyes, the train had stopped. From the corridor came the sound of voices and footsteps. Anvari looked at the other passengers in amazement. "Have we arrived? " he asked.

"The hell we have," said the woman. The man sitting next to the window stifled a yawn.

Anvari looked at his watch. Two hours had passed since the train had started off. "What's happened? " he asked. "Why have we stopped? "

"God knows," said the man next to the window.

The man with the newspaper laughed from behind it. "Calm down, man. It's no use getting upset."

Anvari jumped up.

"What's the idea? " the woman said. "As soon as anything happens you get up and start moving around."

"I'll be right back," said Anvari. "Excuse me." He went into the corridor. The passengers were looking out the window. "What's happened? " he asked. He walked to the end of the corridor and stopped. Shirin-khanom's bird was in his arms. No one had gotten off the train.

He stuck his head into another compartment and asked:

47

"Pardon me, why has the train stopped? " No one knew. Someone said: "Damn them!"

"There must be a reason." said Anvari. "Oh sure!" the man said, and laughed.

Anvari said: "I'm going to go to the information section and ask."

"Shit on their information section!" said the man.

Anvari didn't like that. He stepped out and walked down the corridor.

Someone was banging on the restroom door from the inside. Anvari listened. He looked around him and was afraid. "Who is it? " he called out. "What's happened? " The person was turning the door handle and saying something. Anvari put the bird down and grabbed the handle. He turned it and pulled on it. It was no use. "What's happened? " he asked. The person inside kicked the door and shouted curses. Anvari was stunned. He was upset. He wanted to leave, but he couldn't bring himself to. He said: "I'll push from the outside, and you pull from the inside. " It didn't work. "Don't get upset," he said. "I'm going to go get the ticket inspector right away. " "They all say that!" shouted the man. "Even the ticket inspector!" "I'll be right back," said Anvari, and he rushed away. He opened the door to his compartment and said: "There's someone imprisoned in the bathroom."

"So what's it to us? " said the man next to the door.

"I have to help that poor man locked in there." said Anvari.

"It's not our fault." said the woman.

Anvari went and asked in the other compartments. No one knew where the ticket inspector was. The door at the end of the car was locked. He banged on the window and pulled the doorhandle.

He went back to the restroom door and called out: "I haven't found anyone." There was no answer. He listened and turned the handle. He tapped on the door with his finger. "Mister? " he asked. "Are you still in there? " The man yelled: "Goddamn you, you bastard! Just wait till I get out! I'll show you!"

Anvari felt a heat flash. He felt dizzy for the first time in ages. Even his stomach started aching. He went back to his compartment and opened the door. He shook his head sadly and said: " He might as well stay locked up in there. That's what he deserves."

There was someone sitting in his seat. Anvari looked at the other passengers, and said: "Excuse me, this is my seat. I think there's been a mistake." The old woman said something in Turkish[1] and smacked her lips. "Please excuse me." Anvari said. "I don't know Turkish. This is my seat. " The old woman said something very fast in Turkish. Anvari asked the other passengers if they knew Turkish. The man next to the door shook his head. The man reading the newspaper didn't answer. The woman said: "I understand it but I don't speak it." Anvari cheered up and said: "Could you please tell this lady that this is my seat? " The woman answered: "I told you, I don't know how to speak it."

Anvari apologized: "Yes, yes. I wasn't thinking clearly. Then please tell me what she said. " The woman answered: "She says it's her seat. " Anvari was about to lose his composure, but he controlled himself. "What does she mean it's her seat? There must be some mistake. You are witness to the fact that this is my seat."

The man reading the newspaper said: "Could we have ten minutes of quiet? "

Anvari answered: "Please allow me to straighten out this situation."

"Go complain." said the woman.

The man next to the window started to get up. Anvari started to move back. The woman's knitting needle poked him in the back of his thigh and he cried out. His leg was wavering up in the air and he almost dropped Shirin-khanom's bird. "I'm going to go and bring the official in charge. There are rules and regulations, you know!"

He went out and stood next to the window. Outside there was sun and dust, and lots of boulders and pebbles, hills and gullies. He recalled what Heydari had always said: "You must be strong-hearted and think positively. You must be optimistic and laugh at problems. Whistle and hum a tune. Repeat regularly 'Oh my, what a wonderful day!' and take deep breaths. Every minute, say: 'I'm happy. I'm victorious. Here's to me!'"

Anvari did just that. He pressed his face against the window and said: "My, what a lovely, wonderful day! What a scenic landscape! What a lot of dust! What interesting rocks! What majestic ruins! What gullies!" He turned and looked at the other passengers. He waved to them. He took out his little notebook in which he had recorded several verses of poetry that he could never remember, and recited them under his breath. He tried to memorize them, but couldn't. It was hard. The other passengers in his compartment were eating something together. The old woman was muttering something in Turkish. The other woman had knitted quite a bit. That made Anvari happy, and from the corridor he pointed to the scarf she was knitting and nodded his head admiringly. He wanted to be with them, to talk with them. He knew a few good jokes, and he had a box of *gaz²* in his suitcase. He could get it out and divide it up among them. Or he could do nothing at all, just sit in a corner and be with them, occasionally agree with what they said, and laugh if necessary.

More than half of the passengers had stepped off the train. Anvari picked up the bird, which had been napping, and hurried off too. The ticket inspector was standing over to the side. Anvari cautiously asked him: "Excuse me, where are we?"

"There's no name. It's just wilderness."

"Why have we stopped?"

"How should I know?"

Someone asked: "Where is the conductor?"

Anvari lit up and repeated after him: "Yes, where is the conductor?"

The conductor was nowhere to be found. They thought he might be on the train, so they got back on and looked everywhere. No conductor.

Anvari remembered his ulcer and tried to remain calm. He was hungry, and he hadn't taken his stomach pills. The ticket inspector was cleaning his teeth with a matchstick. Anvari poked his head out the window and asked: "Have they found the conductor?" The inspector pointed to the conductor sitting over to the side.

"Thank God!" said Anvari to himself. He opened the door to the compartment and said breathlessly: "They've found the conductor! He's out there."

He quickly shut the compartment door and stepped off the train. Buttoning his jacket, he approached the conductor and asked: "Are you the conductor? " The man nodded. "Why have we stopped?" asked Anvari, "What's happened?" "It's orders. " replied the conductor.

"Orders? " asked Anvari, and his heart sank. He started to back off and then rushed back onto the train.

Shirin-khanom's bird was growing restless and fidgeting around. A man standing in the corridor next to the window said: "I wish I were a bird, or a dog, or a cat, or any goddamn thing except what I am."

"Did you know that it's orders? " asked Anvari.

"I don't want to know." said the man. "What do I care? All I know is that the train is stopped. Maybe it'll start off again; maybe it never will. Maybe it'll start off and then stop again. Maybe we'll just have to stay right here."

"Yes. Thank you. I understand. " said Anvari.

"Anything's possible." said the man. "Who knows? Who can deny it? Maybe they'll load us all onto a truck and dump us into the river. Maybe. . . "

Anvari stepped aside. He nodded in agreement and then hurriedly walked away. "I'm going to go and speak to the conductor." he said to himself.

He stepped off the train and strode up to the conductor with grim determination.

Several highway patrolmen were standing in front of the train.

Anvari stopped, stunned. Shirin-khanom's bird toppled

out of his hand. He backed away a few steps, then turned and hurriedly got back onto the train. He had a burning sensation at the tip of his stomach; a stubborn pain twisted from the middle of his stomach up to his shoulder.

The other passengers were silent. The old woman had taken some things out of her bundle and was eating. Through the compartment door she offered some to Anvari. The man sitting next to the door got up, came out of the compartment and said to Anvari: "Here. Go and sit in my seat."

Anvari thanked him and cautiously entered the compartment. He was tired and his feet were killing him. He sat down, took the cucumber the old woman was offering him and bit into it sadly. He thought of dinner at Mahdavi's house and felt even sadder. He was thirsty. His jacket smelled of Shirin-khanom's bird.

The old woman pointed at the bird and said something in Turkish. Anvari thought of the patrolmen, of the jeep driving up and down along the road, about the man locked inside the bathroom; he thought about the strange dream he had had, about Mahdavi and his latest picture. He flicked at the geranium plant and pulled off its leaves.

Someone was running down the corridor.

Heydari had said: "It won't be the same old Mahdavi you always knew. He's a stranger now; it's been seven years. If you go, you'll be sorry."

Shirin-khanom had said: "Go ahead. Don't listen to them. Some things are forever, and take root deep inside us." Azizi had said: "With every passing minute one becomes a stranger to oneself, with every thought, with every glance."

The girl had brought out her balloon again.

Anvari said to her: "You blow into that and I'll. . . " The girl started crying. The woman rolled up her knitting and put it down beside her. She leaned over and whispered something into the girl's ear. The man reading the newspaper said: "Aren't you feeling well?"

Anvari stood up. He looked at the other passengers. The pain had reached his armpits. His mouth was dry. The woman moved aside. The old woman was looking at him in silence; only her mouth moved. He stepped out into the corridor, pulled down the window and threw the geranium out. He got off the train. It was getting dark. There was a piece of rock candy in his pocket; he took it out and put it in his mouth. There were some trees along the road. He started walking and tried to remember Heydari's advice. He wanted to whistle, but he didn't know how. He tried to hum, but he didn't have the inclination. The countryside smelled strange, unfamiliar and melancholy. Something heavy hung in the air, like a disaster steadily drawing nearer.

In the shadow of the sunset, the train looked ugly and frightening.

Everyone stood in silence. There was shade under the trees, and Anvari sat down. He undid his tie and threw it on the ground. His trousers were all stained. "If something terrible happens to me," he thought, "no one will ever know. "

A black cab was parked on the side of the road. The driver was waiting for passengers for the trip back.

Anvari snatched his jacket and got up. He picked up Shirin-khanom's bird, looked at it, then changed his mind and threw it onto the ground. He swallowed what was left of the piece of candy and started walking quickly. He waved to the driver and walked faster.

"We're going back. " said the cab driver. "We're going to Tehran. "

Anvari nodded, got into the car and huddled next to the door. He closed his eyes and leaned his head against the back of the seat. He thought of Shirin-khanom, who'd said: "Don't listen to them. Go ahead and go."

"God protect us." said the driver, and he stepped on the gas.

---

1. A large minority of Iranians are native speakers of Turkish.
2. *Gaz* is a traditional Iranian nougat candy, made in the city of Isfahan.

6

Mahdavi tossed and turned, moaned and gasped for breath. He kicked aside the hot, heavy sheets knotted around his body. He opened his eyes and stared with terror into the thick darkness that filled the courtyard. His head beat like a feverish pulse, and it was as if his blood had coagulated in his veins. Something rough, massive and steely weighed on him like an invisible cloak. He breathed with difficulty, and his arms and legs were lost in the darkness. The only feeling in his body was the painful pressure of his heart, which sat in his chest like a huge bird and slowly sucked his blood.

He couldn't remember the dream he had had, but whatever it was its strange taste was still in his mouth, and the dreadful smell of that half-forgotten place in his dream emanated from the depths of the night. Their small courtyard was not the courtyard he knew. It was foreign and unreal, somewhere beyond the boundaries of the intimate and the borders of the familiar. In the garden, even, a thousand black flowers had grown, and the trees rustled in a demonic whisper.

He forced himself to raise his head. He blinked and tried to wake up. He wanted to shake himself, sweep himself off and wash away the filth of that dream and this night of gloom from his soul.

"What an awful nightmare," he said to himself. "It's a good thing I woke up. Thank God."

He reached out, picked up the bowl of icewater near his head and gulped it down. He pressed the cold surface of the bowl against his face, against his neck. He took a piece of ice and held it against his forehead, then his chest, then his stomach. He closed his eyes and tried to ignore the stubborn anxiety that was gradually settling in the pit of his stomach.

"As soon as the sun comes out I'll be fine. " he said to himself. "These fears are part of the night."

He turned over his pillow, which was soaked with perspiration. He shook the noxious little bits of dirt off the mattress from under him. He straightened out the sheet and spread it over his legs. He lay his head down and waited to fall asleep. He was uncomfortable sleeping on his back. He tossed, then turned onto his stomach. He put his right arm under his head, and bent his left arm. Then he picked it up and dangled it off the side of the bed. He wondered where to put it so he'd be comfortable. An extra limb had appeared on his body, and he couldn't remember how he usually slept. He turned onto his side, drew his legs up to his chest, straightened his arms alongside his body, and said: "That's it. This is perfect. "

His fingertips and the soles of his feet burned. He was still thirsty. He felt as if a burning wind whirled in the depths of his soul, and an arid desert stretched under his skin. He licked his parched lips, and looked out of the corner of his eye at Talat-khanom. He was reminded of his half-forgotten dream and felt a twinge in his stomach. He turned away. He pulled the sheet over his head and closed his eyes tightly. His ears were filled with the sound of Talat-khanom's breathing, like the wind risen from the depths of the earth, heavy and hot. He tried not to listen, not to think, to just sleep. He counted from one hundred to two hundred, from two hundred down to one, from one to one thousand. He put his head under the pillow and covered his ears with his hands. "I wish it were morning."

he said to himself. "I wish the sun would come up. "

The hot breath, the sweat and the smell of old feathers stifled him, and he tossed the pillow aside, heaving out the heavy air he'd gulped in with difficulty.

Talat-khanom's arm was stretched out toward him. Her mouth was half open and the tip of her gold tooth shone in the night. She lay motionless, and her face had an animal serenity.

She'd looked the same on her wedding night, serene and tame, like a sated, unaggressive tiger.

The guests had stood at the foot of the stairs. No one spoke. No one was happy, not even Mahdavi.

Talat-khanom was upstairs. From her room came the sounds of shouting and laughter, of tambourines and drums, of sharp scissors, and something like the sound of a saw.

Azizi had said: "The wolf's sharpening her teeth. " The tables were laden with fruit and sweets. No one touched them. Mahdavi sat in front of the wedding mirror[1] and didn't move. His face was ashen and on his tightly closed lips was a grin that frustrated and scared everyone.

Anvari was walking around with a tray of teaglasses, serving the guests. It was as if he had come to his own funeral, and he acknowledged their expressions of sympathy with a sad look. "These things happen. " he'd said. "What can you do? " He'd wanted to say something else, but a hushed murmur from the guests had interrupted him.

Talat-khanom was standing at the top of the stairs. She'd strung lights around her head, little colored ones that blinked on and off, with liquid bubbling inside them. She'd rented her white gown, and it was too short and too tight. Shirin-khanom had made her bouquet with fresh flowers from her own garden. She hadn't changed her shoes; they were the same big men's shoes that were always covered with dust, and that had nails and metal heelplates under the soles that clanged when she walked.

Her mother and maternal aunts had gathered around her on the stairs, and had trilled so stridently that the house had trembled.

The guests had all huddled together, bewildered, not knowing what to do. With every step forward by Talat-khanom the crowd edged backward and breathed louder.

The old women sang congratulatory chants and showered spittle on everyone.

Mahdavi had trembled. He'd wanted to get up, to scream, to run away. But he'd sat, dumbstruck, and stared at Talat-khanom's reflection in the mirror.

Anvari had stood with his head hanging and his lips pouting.

Talat-khanom had burst out laughing. She'd thrown her arm around Mahdavi's waist, stood him up and twirled him around. She'd patted him, kissed him and said: "What's wrong with you? Why are you looking so miserable? Is this a wedding or a funeral?"

Hashemi had said: "Yes, let's get up and clap and dance. " And he'd gotten up. He'd put his hands on his hips and run around the room. He'd twirled. He'd skipped on one leg. He'd tried to liven up the party. He'd jumped up in the air and tried to kick his heels before coming down. He hadn't made it. He'd fallen onto the carpet, flat on his face. He'd knocked his lip on the edge of the table and it had swelled. But in spite of all that he'd laughed. He'd even wanted to sing. But Talat-khanom had stopped him, saying: "Shut up, everyone! I'm going to sing myself."

She'd brought out her *tar*. She'd sat on the carpet and leaned against the wall. The lights on her head blinked and bubbled. Her voice didn't go with her big body: it was calm, weary and sad, like the rustling of the wind in the trees.

Anvari had leaned his head on his knee and cried, quietly, from the bottom of his heart.

Mahdavi tossed and turned again. He tried not to think. He lay on his back. He opened his eyes again and looked at all the black branches above his head. The night was airless, and the bricks in the wall exuded a monstrous heat, like the panting of an old dragon. He sat up and wiped his wet forehead with his hand. He got out of bed and couldn't find his shoes, so he shrugged and started walking barefoot. He was hot. He went and sat on the edge of the fountain pool and took off his clothes. He bent over and stared down into the water. It was cool and fresh, and murmured enticingly; it felt alive and familiar. He ran his hand over the skin of the water, over the gentle concentric ripples waving outward through his fingers. He crept closer and bent over. His breath disturbed the little circles in the water. He stuck out his tongue and ran it over the water's surface. He stretched out his arms and lay his face against the faint ripples. He yearned to slide in, to go down under and never touch the bottom. It seemed to him that the bottom of this pool reached the end of the world, and he yearned for this lovely, cool water to swallow him and take him away.

He turned around and looked at Talat-khanom from the corner of his eye. His heart stopped. It was as if he were seeing that face for the first time: that wild, dampish hair that moved like seaweed, hideously; that hot, dark skin; and that omnivorous, open mouth, that swallowed up the night and with every breath filled the air with a hellish decay. He remembered that day, the first day, the day it all began. He was sitting in the courtyard with Anvari, playing backgammon. Each had won three games, each had lost three games, and as usual they were even. Heydari had looked at the red socks and striped pajama-bottoms[2] they were both wearing and laughed: "How nice!" he'd said. "What togetherness. It warms my heart."

Mahdavi was feeling happy too. He'd scratched himself and laughed. He'd stretched out on his back on the carpet next to the flowerbed, and let the autumn afternoon sun gradually put him to sleep. He was happy that he could just stretch out like a lazy kitten and not think about anything or feel anything, just draw a total blank. However, like someone who suddenly senses danger, he'd opened his eyes. There was something invisible but tangible wafting through the air.

He'd sat up, spellbound. He was sure that someone else besides him was there, nearby. Behind him was their house, with the closed windows, the green netting and Anvari's clothes hanging on the clothesline. To the left was the same old vacant lot. Straight ahead was the wall, the street, and a rundown old building with dust-covered windows and balconies filled with broken tables and chairs, tin cans, empty bottles and old newspapers. Farther over was the streetlamp and the only tree on the street, and another window. That's where she was. In the frame of that window there was someone standing, staring at him, and with that stare it was as if her entire soul, like a mass of compressed air that has suddenly found an outlet, was rushing out through the pupils of her eyes.

Mahdavi had quickly turned away and started biting his nail. He'd turned the radio up louder than ever; he'd started flipping through the pages of the newspaper repeating each line out loud to himself. He'd gotten up and walked around, talking out loud. He'd watered the garden, and looked out of the corner of his eye at that old dust-covered window, and wondered: "Where have I seen that woman? How do I know her? "

Anvari had said: "I don't know her."

Heydari had said: "Yes, I know who she is. She's not the kind of person we would associate with. I've arranged to have her removed from the neighborhood."

"She's a disgrace," Azizi had said.

"Yes, I agree," Mahdavi had said. "We should make sure she is thrown out of here, by all means." And he'd calmed down. He felt reassured that everything was back in its place and that his languid afternoon naps would again be undisturbed.

The next day he'd tried not to look at that window, but he had. The day after he'd tried not to think about the woman behind that window, but he had. Every day after that he'd tried not to go into the street, but he had. He'd looked at Anvari, at Heydari, at himself, thinking: "What if they find out? What if they catch me one day?"

The friends had gradually caught on too. Anvari had noticed before everyone else, and had told Heydari.

They were at Hashemi's house.

Anvari, pale and embarrassed, was hunched up in a corner, saying nothing. Heydari, his eyes shifting and his voice suspicious, had said: "Well, Mahdavi-jan, you haven't told us where you were all last night. Hmm? "

"We were worried. " Hashemi had said. "We'd thought—God forbid—that something had happened to you."

"We went to all the hospitals." Azizi had said. "We called a hundred police stations. You see, you had never just taken off without letting anyone know!"

Shirin-khanom had laughed. She'd looked at him with kindness. She'd leaned over and whispered into his ear: "I know where you were. Good for you. Don't listen to anyone."

Mahdavi had blushed. He'd bowed his head and scratched himself. He'd said: "I went for a walk. I wasn't feeling too well."

The friends had looked at each other, and Mahdavi had said to himself: "I won't go anymore. It's finished."

But he'd gone again, two nights later. He'd bunched up his blanket so Anvari wouldn't notice he was gone. He'd carried his shoes under his arm and put his clothes on out in the street. It was almost morning when he'd returned, tiptoeing and nervous. With his shoes and clothes on he'd crept under his blanket, and tried to breathe regularly and calmly.

Anvari had pretended to be asleep, but through the mosquito net he'd seen Mahdavi's eyes, and cringed. In those eyes was a gleam that hadn't been there before, and the depths of those anxious pupils were filled with unfamiliar emotion, with wonder, with entrancing temptations, and with the awe of a new experience. Anvari realized that something far beyond what he'd imagined had happened to his friend. What? He didn't know. He could only sense it; he sensed that it was something aberrant, and he shuddered.

Mahdavi had closed his eyes and pressed his head against the pillow, happy to be back, in his own bed, with his own familiar breaths, dreams, thoughts and plans. He'd felt happy that the world was the same old reasonable world, and that he was the same old Mahdavi, with his goals, his lifestyle, his beliefs, and his friends. He'd said to himself: "Thank God! Whatever it was, it's over. I'll never go again. " He'd slept soundly. And he'd awakened refreshed, as always. He'd listened to the water boiling in the samovar, to the old streetsweeper grumbling in the street, to the sounds coming from Anvari's radio and to the clinking of the tea-glasses. He'd gotten up. He'd said hello to the neighbor who was watering his garden, and had inquired about the health of his wife and children and about his stomach ailment. He'd stood next to Anvari and they'd done their exercises; they'd jogged around the courtyard ten times, and taken twelve deep breaths. They'd taken a shower and scrubbed each other's backs, and laughed.

At eight o'clock, just like every other day, they were at their desks. They'd called Heydari and Azizi and Hashemi, asking them about their health and telling them how they were. They had both received a monthly raise of one hundred and fifty-six tomans. [3] They'd congratulated each other and kissed each other on the cheek. The company employees had clapped for them, and they'd sent the servant out to buy cake and ice cream for everybody. And they'd thanked God from the bottom of their hearts.

Heydari had told them: "I'm proud of both of you. I pray to God you will always be successful."

They'd gone back home. Mahdavi had packed his things to go to the baths. He'd said. "I want to wash myself clean from head to toe."

In the street, he'd whistled. He'd looked at the newly paved road with joy, and thanked the neighborhood policeman for his vigilance and dedication. But before getting to the baths, at the corner, he'd stopped, and felt his legs were shaking. "What is it?" he'd wondered. "What's wrong with me? Why is my head feeling hot? Why is my heart pounding like this? " He'd held on to the handle of his bag tightly and tried to walk faster. But he'd noticed that he was standing there, nailed down, helpless. "What's going on? Why am I just standing here? Why have I stopped breathing? Why am I shaking? "

Then he'd seen himself turn around, go right, then turn left, then run. "I'll go back to Heydari's house. " He'd said to himself. "I'll go back to the office. I'll go to the movies..." Then he'd looked up, and seen that he was right back in front of that old broken brown door, ringing the doorbell, going upstairs. He'd seen that he was in that steamy, darkened room, facing Talat-khanom, in her arms, against her bosom, under her hair, and he'd realized that he was melting, crumbling, cutting loose from all the moments that had been and would be, from all the "shoulds" and the "musts"; and he had laughed, heartily, like when he was a child and everything was a game; then he'd lost track of all that too, and after that he hadn't seen or thought of anything more.

But then he'd awakened again, not knowing how many hours or days had passed. He'd sat up in bed and looked at Talat-khanom horrified, at the filthy curtains covered with dust, at the unfamiliar walls, at the things around the room that smelled strange and foreign, and at himself. He'd felt scared. He'd remembered Anvari, and his bath kit; he'd remembered his pay raise and the new title he'd been waiting for. He'd remembered his friends and Heydari who'd said: "I'm proud of both of you."

He'd wrenched his hand from Talat's. He'd cursed her, kicked her door, kicked her petunia plant, her sewing machine and her radio. "What do you want from me? " he'd screamed. "Why don't you leave me alone?"

He'd lept into the street and run all the way home. He'd leaned against the wall and watched the children coming noisily out of school. He'd watched the plump, healthy women returning from the baths; they were pregnant and their arms were filled with bread, fruit and fresh greens. He'd walked around the square near his house, along with the men coming home from work, some running after taxis and others standing in line for the bus, shifting their weight from one leg to the other. He'd wished he could be with them, with these people whose conversations were polite, dignified and precise, about daily tribulations and concrete fears, about small, limited goals and easily achieved happinesses, about well-known diseases and common aches and pains, about natural desires and conventional loves, about people who were with them, looked like them, and had the same-colored briefcases and hats and shoes.

He'd bought two lottery tickets from the blind ticket-seller on the corner of his street, and a magazine from the newspaper man. He'd tipped his hat with respect to the landlord's wife and had bowed to her from afar. Then he'd jumped into his house and locked the door, breathing a sigh of relief. He'd felt that he was back in his own skin again, back in his little circle where all points were the same distance from the center, and where nothing threatened his simple order of things.

He'd gone to the movies with Anvari. They'd dropped into Heydari's cousin's store and looked at all his carpets. They'd gone to Hashemi's house and they had all laughed together. They'd talked, read the newspaper and drunk pepsi.

They'd sat in front of the TV, and Mahdavi had said to himself: "How wonderful to always be with one's friends, safe and secure."

But a few nights later he'd awakened again, stifled, burning and restless, soaked in sweat. It had seemed to him that someone was calling his name from a distance, from behind the trees, from the depth of the night. He'd turned and looked with horror behind him, around him, under the bed and in the courtyard. He'd felt the presence of someone familiar next to him, someone hot and quivering, and the disturbing smell of her hair wafted through the air.

He'd held his nose and writhed in his bed, weak and helpless. The smell robbed him of his rest and peace of mind, and the memory of something indefinite made his heart tremble. It was a smell that exuded from the darkest recesses of his being—the smell of his mother's henna'd hair, the smell of his father's mouth when he'd drunk vodka and gone after his uncle's wife in the dark hallway, the frightening smell of Bibi-khanom in the basement of his grandfather's house, the smell of Zan-agha when she'd given birth, when she'd been beaten by her husband and was crying in the bathroom. It was the smell of all these things, and was none of them.

He'd put his head under the pillow and bitten the corner of the mattress. "I'm not going to budge. " he'd said. He'd groaned, tossed and turned and fluttered. He'd sat up and said. "I'm not going. I'm not going. No way. " He'd started walking, then running. He'd knocked on the door and gone inside. He'd put his head on Talat-khanom's lap and kissed her knees. He'd sniffed and chewed at her hair, and like a parched fish that has found water again he'd let himself go. He'd given himself up to the darkness of this greedy torrent and to a thousand other unknown sensations; and he'd realized that he was dying, shedding his skin, disintegrating, and along with all the ancient winds and roots he was passing under the world and returning to the beginning, to that black, perfect night.

Heydari had said: "Just leave him there. He's beyond redeeming himself."

Azizi had said: "He'll never come back."

But he had come back, tired, distressed and feverish, like someone returning from a dangerous journey, like a sick man who has barely recovered from a near-fatal illness. He'd taken off his shoes at the door, his shirt in the garden, and his trousers at the foot of the stairs. He'd cried, in front of Anvari and Heydari. His upper lip was swollen; he had a black eye and his ear was all bloody.

He'd turned to Anvari and said: "Anvari-jan, take me away from here, before it's too late, while there's still a chance."

Anvari had agreed to. He'd cradled Mahdavi's head and helped him fall asleep. He'd brought his dinner for him in bed and washed his ear off with warm water.

They'd packed their suitcases. Anvari had rented a cab. They'd arranged to go to Meygoon, to Hashemi's uncle's house.

Heydari had said: "Be careful of your money. Don't lose it."

Azizi had said: "If only you had thought of this sooner. "

They'd gotten into the cab. They'd put their suitcases in the trunk, and their magazines, backgammon set and boxes of nuts and candy in the front seat.

Mahdavi had said: "My! What wonderful sunshine!" He'd waved to his friends and they'd smiled. Anvari had brought two straw hats, one for himself and one for Mahdavi; they were wearing them.

Hashemi had held up the Koran for them to pass under.[4] He'd given them two pictures of Shirin-khanom to take to his uncle. "See," he'd said, "God willing everything works out for the best."

Mahdavi had said: "My sunglasses! What have I done with my sunglasses?"

They'd looked on the floor of the cab and under their things. "I've left them behind." he'd said. "Wait, I'll be right back."

He hadn't come back. Not that day, not that night, not that week, nor the month after.

Something was moving at the bottom of the water, and the night, heavy and damp, stood among the trees. Mahdavi turned away and shuddered: "What is it that ties me to this woman? What got me so involved with her?"

He got up. He yearned for Anvari. He looked at Talat-khanom from afar, and something like a bullet, a clap of thunder, shot through his head.

"I wish she'd die." he thought. "I wish she'd somehow disappear."

He looked at a rock next to the flowerbed and shuddered. He quickly turned away and tried to think of something nice and simple and wholesome. He thought back to the nights when he and Anvari would sleep on the roof, and the only thing that would disturb their rest was the buzz of mosquitoes and the neighbors' quarreling. He thought back to the weekends: he and Anvari would go hiking; they'd eat lunch by the riverside and nap all afternoon. They'd planned to get married at the same time, have children at the same time, put their money in the same bank account, retire together, grow old together, and die together. They'd planned to buy two plots in Emamzadeh Saleh[5] and share the same gravestone.

He stood up. His heart was fluttering like a frantic bird. He walked around the pool. The trees had grown taller, and there were suspicious shadows everywhere that moved and were alive.

"I'll kill her. " he said to himself, and his body felt hot. He came and stood over Talat-khanom and looked at her. His ears were filled with strange sounds. An invisible hand clawed at his heart. It was as if it wanted to wrench something from the depths of his being and throw it out. He bent over and picked up the rock next to the flowerbed. His lips were tight and he breathed with difficulty. Again that hatred-filled nausea had seized him. It had started that day next to the garage. Talat-khanom's mother had had a sheep slaughtered in front of their car.[6] She had dipped her hand in the blood and rubbed it all over their back fender. Then she'd wrapped the warm, bloody liver in a handkerchief and handed it to Mahdavi, saying: "Plant it in your garden; it will bring abundance."

Mahdavi had looked at the sheep's severed head and wide-open eyes, at the mass of flies crawling over the carcass, at the bloody liver wrapped in the handkerchief on his lap, at Talat-khanom and her red hair, at the long and dusty road that stretched out before them, at the shamed looks of his friends, and suddenly he'd felt sick. He'd thrown up, all over himself and Talat-khanom's skirt and the bouquet of flowers Anvari had brought him as a present. He'd leaned his head on Talat-khanom's shoulder and looked at Anvari, like someone who is asleep, like someone staring incredulously at the corpse of a dear one, like someone realizing for the first time that someday he will die.

He turned away. He put the rock he was holding back down. He bent over and fell to his knees. "I'll choke her. I'll throw her into the pool. " he said to himself. He crept closer, on his hands and knees. He put his hands on the edge of the bed and lifted himself up.

Talat-khanom was sleeping on her back. Her face was towards the sky, and the moon was right above it. She didn't move, and her breathing could no longer be heard.

Mahdavi crept closer. The sheets had bunched up and

wound around his arms and legs. The bed had become as wide as the world, and getting over to the other side seemed to take as long as Noah lived.

"Maybe I'm sick. " he'd said to Anvari. "What can I say? Even I don't know what's wrong with me. But whatever it is it will come to an end. My place isn't with that woman."

To Heydari he had said: "Yes, you're right. One must have willpower. One must be firm, and persist. Life is as simple as two plus two equals four."

To Shirin-khanom he had said: "With you one forgets one has problems and sorrows. One feels that one is still a child, still sweet and naughty."

He listened. The whole city was asleep. He stretched out his weary arms and dragged himself onto Talat-khanom. His fingertips burned, and something in his being wanted to pour out from the palms of his hands.

"I'm going to kill her." he said to himself. "This time I'm really going to kill her."

He drew himself up, grabbed Talat-khanom's throat in his hands, and trembled.

The trees were watching him from afar. The wind stood still upon the wall, waiting. Talat-khanom, her eyes wide open, was looking at him, with calm and kindness. She wasn't surprised; she wasn't afraid. She was willing, submissive, and happy. It was as if she had known beforehand, and had been waiting for this moment.

Mahdavi tried not to look at her. He closed his eyes and squeezed harder. He had trouble breathing. His mouth gaped and his temples were pounding. He could feel Talat-khanom's breath on his face, on his lips. The protruding vein on her neck pulsated slowly. From her hair, from between her eyelids, from all the pores of her skin exuded that heat, that magic, soporific heat.

Mahdavi sensed that his hands weren't moving and that his fingers no longer had that deadly strength. "I'm going to kill her." he'd said. "Right now. While there's still a chance." But his hands were no longer under his control; they obeyed another law. His thoughts spinned inside his head like concentric ripples on water, and faded away. His mind was again filled with confusion and turmoil, and a strange temptation scattered the structure of his rational thoughts. Talat-khanom's heartbeat sounded as if it were coming from the heart of the earth, and her body was like a huge black pit that sucked everything into itself.

Mahdavi muttered something unintelligible and huddled against Talat-khanom. He lay his head between her breasts and lost all train of thought.

The sun was rising when Talat-khanom got up. She lifted Mahdavi's head and gently lay it on the pillow. She drew the sheet up to his shoulders and listened to his even breathing. She got out of bed. She picked up her *chador*[7] that had fallen on the ground, rolled up her sleeves, and performed the ablutions for the morning prayer.

---

1. In a traditional Iranian wedding ceremony, the bride and groom sit before a wedding mirror and a pair of candelabra.

2. At home, Iranians wear loose-fitting flannel or cotton trousers for comfort. The English word "pajama" is derived from a Persian word meaning "leg-garment. "

3. About $22.00.

4. Traditional custom to invoke protection for someone setting off on a journey.

5. A shrine in the mountains above Tehran.

6. It is customary to sacrifice a sheep on happy occasions, in order to give thanks and invoke divine protection.

7. A *chador* is a full-length veil.

7

I clear away the dinner dishes and put them on top of the plates piled over against the wall from last night. I fill the tea kettle with water and put it on the heater. My pack of cigarettes is on the shelf; it only has two cigarettes left. Oh well, I'll have one with my tea, and save the other for when I get into bed, when I've turned out the light, when, between those cold sheets and that dense darkness, my loneliness is greater than ever.

I take a walk around the room, around the furniture and the heater. This is my nightly routine, before I go to bed: ten times, twelve times around the room or more.

There is so much dust everywhere, on the windows, the table, the lightbulb, the sheets, on me, on this room. Where does it come from? Not from the outside. Outside there's only snow and wind. And the doors are closed. It's from in here. It comes from me, from my gaze, my breath, my skin, from my dusty imagination.

"Aren't you afraid of dying?" I asked Jalili.

"I'm afraid of ending, of dropping dead like a cow. " he answered.

Ahmadi said: "I'm terrified of living."

Hashemi said: "Let's not talk like this. What's the idea? "

Shirin-khanom said: "Dying is a kind of going. You can't just stay in one place."

She had her suitcase in her hand. "Where to? " I asked. "Are you planning to take a trip?"

"We're going to the seashore," she said. "It'll be good for her," said Hashemi. "She'll get her health back. " He smiled. He was happy. He'd gone to the barber and had his hair parted in the middle like Heydari. His left eye was swollen shut. His nose was swollen too, and his cheek was all scratched up.

"It's nothing," he said. "I fell down."

Shirin-khanom whispered into my ear: "He's lying. His students pushed him down. They booed him and jeered at him. They came up from behind and poured water all over his new clothes."

But he wasn't upset. "They're good kids," he said. "They just wanted to play a prank on me. " He'd been beaten up another time too, I remember. He was working nights, saying: "I want to take Shirinak[1] to the seashore. I don't have any money; they haven't paid me my salary. It's not that they don't want to, but. . . well, they just haven't paid me yet. They must not have the money. " He added "Don't tell anyone where I work. I wouldn't want anyone to know."

I went to see him. In a park behind their house were a swing, a slide, and a merry-go-round. There was also a place called the Tunnel of Terror, a dark, winding corridor.

"Hashemi-jan," I'd said, "is that you? " I couldn't believe my eyes. He'd been turned into a skeleton: they'd stuffed him into a gunnysack down to his waist with only his legs sticking out, and they'd painted a skeleton on the sack. His job was to hide in a corner of the Tunnel of Terror, and then leap out and scare people as they went through.

"I keep worrying my students will recognize me. " he said. "I keep praying no one will come by here. I can't bear to scare people."

A few nights later he showed up at my door. It was late. He

70

stood behind the rainspout and mumbled unintelligibly. "What is it?" I asked. "What's happened? Why don't you speak up?" His face and head were all bloody. He said: "It just isn't right to leap out at people and scare them. That's not clean fun. They had a right to get angry." He'd been beaten up by three or four drunken hoodlums, who'd said to him: "Not even God himself ever jumped out and tried to scare us, let alone an old goose like you!"

I remember the day they were leaving for the Caspian seashore. Shirin-khanom looked at me from behind the window of the bus. She looked changed: like a child who's suddenly grown old. I shuddered, remembering the day she was splashing in the fountain-pool.

She was radiant, shining. She was like a violet. One didn't dare go too close, for fear one's breath might wither her translucent skin. I remember Hashemi always murmuring: "Who knows who you really are? Where have you been until now?"

We'd gotten used to not asking. The important thing was that she'd come, that she'd found us. Heydari was the only one who was always wanting to see her identification papers, who was just never satisfied.

How I miss them, all of them. How many times have I looked at that picture on the shelf? Looking at that picture is something I do every night. Sometimes I forget what they looked like; their faces blend into each other in my mind. Heydari looks at me with Shirin-khanom's eyes. Talat-khanom appears with several arms, accompanied by a combination of Mahdavi and Anvari. Whichever one I think of, the other one is there too, imposing his presence.

Last night I dreamed of Mahdavi. Where were we? I don't remember. What were we doing? I can't remember that either. I just know that we were together the whole night. I miss him so much. I miss his round face and his red nose, his rosy cheeks and his pink ears. I miss his childish stubbornness and his incredible laziness.

His death was simple, like he was. He fell into the pool in

his courtyard and drowned. He'd become entangled among the old weeds and the mud at the bottom.

What a trip. I wish we hadn't gone. Jalili said: "Our visit has brought misfortune. How can we face Talat-khanom now?"

We'd arrived the night before, and still hadn't rested from the trip when it happened. We couldn't believe it, Jalili and I. We stood next to the courtyard door and just couldn't go forward. "Maybe we're dreaming," we said, "maybe all this is a game."

His voice was still in our ears. He was present. Death just couldn't be so easy, so insolent and arbitrary.

Talat-khanom had laid him on the cobblestones in the courtyard, under a tree next to the garden. She gazed at him. She crawled around him, sniffing him, calling to him gently. She wrang out his jacket and howled. She wouldn't let us get close, or touch him. She leaned over to protect him from the sun. She held his head and waved the flies away from his face.

How is it we went to Gorgan? I don't remember. One day we just got on the train and went, Jalili and I. There was someone else with us. Who? I don't remember.

I'd said to Jalili: "You knock on the door. I don't dare."

She was a good woman, better than she seemed. She opened the door cautiously, looked through the crack with one eye and stared at us. "What is it? " she said. "What do you want? "

We asked how Mahdavi was. She didn't answer. She stuck her head out and peered into the street. "Anvari isn't with you? " she asked.

We wanted to turn back; she didn't let us. She swore at us and said: "What's wrong with you? Why are you standing there staring at me?"

She grabbed our suitcases and tossed them into the courtyard. Yet that evening she cooked us a good dinner. She even played her *tar* and drank vodka to our health, talking and laughing until midnight. When we slept she watched over us; just before dawn she came and pulled the covers up around Jalili, and gently sprayed mosquito repellant around my bed.

She buried Mahdavi herself. There was no one else in the

cemetary besides us, and it was raining lightly. The wind puffed out her *chador*. She looked grander than ever, like a sad, ancient bird. She didn't cry, at least not in front of us. We couldn't see her face, just her hand that would occasionally come out of her *chador* and claw at the earth on the grave.

"I bathed him today." she said. "He wouldn't let me scrub him down, so I hit him, and then he wouldn't speak to me. He just said that he was going to leave me. I didn't believe him. He went and wrote a long letter to Anvari. I cajoled him, told him I adored him, threw myself at his feet. It was no use. He still wouldn't speak to me. He died without speaking to me."

We went back to the house. She stood next to the fountain-pool and gazed intently into the water, at the ripples on the surface, at the mud in the footbath. The pupils of her eyes had dilated. Her upper lip quivered like the snout of a rabid dog, and the tips of her white teeth gleamed. She didn't look like herself; she didn't look like anyone we knew. It seemed like a face we'd seen in a dream, or an illustration in a book, or the image we'd formed of a woman whose story had once been told to us.

She turned and looked at us: "Why are you standing at the door?"

"We'd better tell Heydari." I said.

She'd taken off her chador. Her black dress, like her wedding gown, was short and tight. She brought us tea, and worried about what we'd have for lunch. She picked up Mahdavi's shoes next to the door, dusted them, and put them under the bed.

"A friend who only comes half way is of no use. " she said. "We both stared at the door 'til our eyes went dry, and still Anvari never came."

There was a knock at the door. It was the neighbors; they'd come to console her. She didn't let them in; she shut the door in their faces and muttered insults at them. On the way back in she gathered the sheets off the clothesline, folded them and put them on the bed on the porch. "If Anvari had come, this wouldn't have happened." she said.

"We'd better be going." said Jalili.

She picked up our suitcases, and wouldn't let us take them from her. She came with us to the street corner, and had us pass under the Koran. She hugged us and kissed us on the forehead.

"Talat-khanom," I asked, "what is there we can do?"

She laughed: "Whenever there's something, I'll let you know."

She never did. I wrote to her many times; she never answered. Jalili and I went to the post office and placed a call to Gorgan; no one answered. We made inquiries, and were told that she'd left that address a long time ago.

I stand next to the window. What snow! What frightening whiteness! There's no one out there. Across from my room there is a window; there's a cement wall and a row of closed windows. What's happened? It's as if everyone has left this city, or died, or turned to stone. Perhaps life, passing by so hurriedly, has forgotten my little room. The wind scatters the snow, hanging onto the iced-over wires, rubbing against my window. Someone has passed through this street; his footprints are in the snow. He's come from behind the vacant lot, crossed the street and returned, standing beneath my window and pacing aimlessly. His footprints next to the wall are hesitant and irregular, as if he'd been looking for someone.

Who could it have been, walking beneath my window? The snow is covering the hollows of his footprints. Maybe he was looking for my address. Tomorrow I'll sit next to the window and look out. Tomorrow. Always waiting for tomorrow. But this tomorow is different from all the other tomorrows. It's always possible that this tomorrow may be the last.

I return to my place next to the heater, pour myself some strong tea, and sit down. The cuckoo in the clock starts squawking for no reason. Sometimes days go by and it doesn't make a sound. Sometimes it'll poke its head out every ten minutes and sing. I don't mind it. We've grown used to each other.

If I didn't have these memories, what would I do? How would I spend these evenings? Each night, one of them has his

74

turn: Hashemi, Mahdavi, Anvari, Shirin-khanom, Heydari. I can't bear to think about Jalili. Maybe I'm scared.

"That guy is different from the rest of us." said Azizi. "He's a different breed."

"You're all afraid of him because he ruins your sweet dreams," said Asgari, "because he sees right through you."

"We have to wait 'til life teaches him a lesson. " said Heydari.

We were at Jalili's house. His father-in-law was there too, sitting at the upper end of the room and reminiscing about his trip abroad.

"He makes me sick." said Jalili. "I wish I could just kick him right out of here."

"What a respectable family!" said Heydari. "Our friend here is really lucky!"

"Come on, Jalili-jan," I said, "you should be more reasonable. You can't change the world single-handedly."

"I'll do what I have to do. " he answered.

He was serious. He never joked with anyone. I still remember that day we ran after him in the street, the day we realized what thoughts lurked in his little head, and we feared the worst.

"What's wrong with all of you?" said Heydari. "Have you gone crazy? Why are you all failing me one by one? "

Shirin-khanom was darting back and forth like a wildcat, grabbing everyone by the collar.

"Shirin-khanom," I said, "we're Jalili's friends. We want to help him. "

She jumped at me and clawed my face. "Why did you lock him in the basement?" she screamed. She bit Hashemi's hand, pulled off her wedding ring, and threw it into the street, saying: "Now I really know you all. I don't love you anymore. "

I wanted to hold her, to keep her. Hashemi knelt in a corner of the room. He held his head in his hands and didn't know what to do.

No. I don't want to think about Jalili. I wish I could wipe all the memories of him from my mind, like the steam on my window.

I get up. I put the kettle, the teapot and the teaglasses over next to the dishes. I take my bedtime pills. I turn off the light and get into bed. I haven't forgotten my cigarette, my only bedtime companion. Oh, it's so cold! I gather up my legs and hold my knees to my chest; I press my hands together. I close my eyes, and listen. Even the rats are asleep.

Back then at least the patrolling policeman would whistle. I used to call him and he'd come in. He was skinny and had a thin moustache. He was happy to be a policeman, to wear laced-up shoes, to blow his whistle and to have a jacket with lots of buttons. He'd say that his father had been a thief, that his brother was a thief, and that his cousin had killed someone and been hanged. He'd stand next to the window and hold his hat to his chest, saying: "But me, dear sir, I've got pride. I'm working for my country." He'd be up all night, even during the freezing winter nights. I'd hear his footsteps beneath my window.

I shut my eyelids tightly. I'm scared, and an unfamiliar feeling warns me. Old man, maybe this is your last night. So maybe I'd better not sleep; maybe I'd better keep track of every moment down to the dregs of time, my time, that passes by with such indifference, and steals everything from me so unfairly. How strange it is not to be waiting for anything, anything at all. The world is totally empty, empty of space, of time, of me. "Old man, tuck your head under the blanket and go to sleep. Old man, watch out. Old man . . ."

---

1. Affectionate diminutive for "Shirin."

8

Everyone's here: the Friends, his father and brother, his paternal aunt, and the neighbors. Milling around Jalili's bed, looking at him, tiptoeing, whispering in each other's ear. They're bewildered and disturbed.

From the hall comes the sound of talking, of weeping, and of breaking sugar.[1]

Someone is pacing the courtyard outside Jalili's window, watching the door. He coughs raspingly, and occasionally kicks the water sprinkler next to the wall.

Jalili's brother hurriedly closes the windows. Someone is searching for something under the bed.

No one speaks. They just look, at each other, and at Jalili, surreptitiously, cautiously, from the corner of their eyes.

"Hurry! Close the curtains!" says someone.

Jalili's father is sitting on the edge of his chair, bewildered and dumbstruck. He doesn't even blink. His hand, holding a glass of tea, remains suspended in mid-air. The lump of sugar he put in his mouth still bulges in his cheek. He doesn't take his eyes off the flower pattern in the carpet.

Azizi is watching the street through a slit in the curtains.

Someone is carefully examining Jalili's books, one by one.

Shirin-khanom is here too, next to Jalili's bed. Her lower lip is gently quivering. Her hand is on Jalili's wet hair, caressing his face. She looks unbelievingly at Jalili's wife, at Azizi, at Hashemi, at Jalili's father, at the neighbors, and then back at Jalili. She can't understand what has happened, and is sad and frightened and hurt. She doesn't like this game. Helpless and bewildered, she looks at Jalili's bound hands and feet and doesn't know what to do. Since this morning she has asked a thousand times: "What is it? What's happened? Why have you tied him up? Why have you gagged him?"

No one has answered.

Hashemi is sadder than everyone else. He has brought blessed sweets and holy water and a jar of fig jam he made himself for Jalili. It's his handkerchief they've used to gag Jalili, his clean and freshly ironed handkerchief scented with rosewater. He has served tea to everyone, asked everyone how they are, and watched that no one's cigarette ashes fall on the carpet.

There are two neighbors, sitting in the hall across from each other. The small plates they hold on their laps are filled with pomegranates, apples, bananas, nuts, two pieces of bologna and some *sowhan* candy.[2] They haven't touched anything. They hang their heads, and only occasionally get up halfway and steal a glance at Jalili.

From the street come the sounds of footsteps and talking. Jalili's wife interrupts what she's been saying and looks with fear at Jalili's brother. Her eyes are red; she's been crying all day and all last night. She looks at Jalili, then at Azizi, then around her.

The sound grows louder and nearer.

Jalili's father, like someone who has abruptly awakened afraid and confused, listens to the voices. He swallows, and quickly chews the sugar cube. "What is it? " he asks. "Who is it?"

"They've come," says Jalili's wife.

Jalili's brother holds his finger to his lips and tiptoes.

78

They look outside with Azizi through the closed curtains. It's dark out in the street. The sound of footsteps fades.

Hashemi gathers up the tea glasses.

Jalili's wife bursts into tears, and the keyring with the keys to all the closets clinks in the cleft of her bosom. "Now what should we do? " she says, leaning against the wall and staring at Jalili in bewilderment. She cannot believe it; frantically she bites at the skin of her lip, and looks at herself in the mirror out of the corner of her eye.

"Maybe it's all a dream," she says, "a nightmare. " She shakes her head. With her nail she presses against the pimple next to her lip and rubs saliva on it. Then, with tired and indifferent eyes, she stares back at Jalili. "Why?" she asks. "How could you? For what?"

Hashemi is worried about Shirin-khanom, about everyone. One of his paintings is hanging on the wall; it's a seascape with some birds and a clear, serene sky.

Jalili's wife pounds against her husband's bed with her fist. Everyone looks at her. The neighbors look in, and whisper something to each other. Azizi shakes his head. Jalili's wife screams. The neighbors stand up and hold tightly onto their plates. They've eaten the bananas and the *sowhan* candy.

Everyone talks to each other. Everyone talks to Jalili's wife at the same time. Everyone looks at Jalili's father who is shouting. Everyone falls silent.

The neighbors have stepped inside the room and are standing next to the door.

Shirin-khanom tries to untie Jalili's hands. She can't. She bends over and tries to loosen the knot with her teeth.

Jalili's father lowers his voice. He's panting. His asthma is back, and some huge mosquito has stung him on the face. "Everyone must remain calm, like me," he says. "Everyone must act as if there is absolutely nothing out of the ordinary." He scratches the large red insect bite on his face, and with a voice that sounds as if it's coming out of the bottom of a well says: "We have to behave in such a way that if anyone comes in, they'll think this is a friendly gathering, a party. We're all just laughing and having a good time."

He goes and brings out his *santur*[3] from behind the curtain. He blows on it and dusts it off with his sleeve.

The neighbors return to their places. They look all around for fruitknives and napkins to eat the pomegranates. They can't find any.

The face of Ammeh-jan Batul[4] moves behind the glass door of the storage room. Something other than eyes gleam behind her grey-tinted glasses.

She looks as if she's laughing. Her yellow teeth are many and long.

Someone is knocking. Jalili's wife jumps. The person outside the window bangs against the window pane. Jalili's brother tries to coax Shirin-khanom away from Jalili's bedside.

Someone is knocking at the door, louder and louder, with determination.

Jalili's father pounds away at his *santur* a few times, saying: "We've got to keep calm. As if nothing's happened. " Azizi opens the window and talks to the person in the courtyard. From behind the storage room door, Ammeh-jan Batul says: "You'd better take him away from here. I've warned you. The devil's gotten into his soul. It'll spread to all of you. "

The knocking becomes insistent.

Jalili's father hurriedly starts playing something dissonant and muddled.

Hashemi, on all fours, is looking behind the sofa for a lost spoon.

The person in the courtyard keeps pounding against the window pane.

"We have no choice. " says Azizi. "We have to open the door." He buttons his jacket, swallows a sneeze and wearily looks at his watch. He's grown heavier than ever, and his hands are covered with liver spots—his latest ailment. He takes a handful of pills out of his pocket, tosses them into his mouth and gulps them down.

Asgari is on top of the roof. He calls down through the furnace pipe. "It's Heydari. Open the door."

Hashemi raises his head and comes out from behind the sofa. Smilingly he holds up the teaspoon he's finally retrieved and shows it to everyone.

Heydari's voice comes from the courtyard, then from the hallway, then from behind the door.

The neighbors greet him with their mouths full. Ammeh-jan Batul presses her face against the glass door. She chants incantations and blows into the room.[5]

Hashemi rushes to move a chair up for Heydari from the corner of the room. He places it next to Jalili's bed. Everyone is looking at Heydari.

Jalili's father plucks at the strings of his *santur* with his fingernail, and sadly looks at Heydari, pointing to his son.

"It's truly strange," says Heydari. "It's unbelievable."

Jalili's wife fetches the tray of fruit which is in front of the neighbors and sets it before Heydari. "See," she says, "he finally did it."

Jalili's father is waving the *santur* sticks in mid-air. He is breathing more heavily, and the insect bite on his face has swollen. "If there were anything he'd been deprived of in life, I wouldn't be so upset. At least I'd understand why he's suddenly lost his mind, why he's committed this terrible sin against himself and all of us."

Shirin-khanom frowns in a corner. She looks at everyone as if she's never seen these faces before.

Azizi loosens his shoelaces. He has heartburn, and he hasn't brought his pain pills. He lets out a broad yawn, along with a stifled moan. A handful of gold teeth shine from inside the dark cavity of his mouth.

Ammeh-jan Batul is now sitting in the frame of the storage room door, mumbling unintelligibly under her black *chador*.

Heydari peers at Jalili, like a scientist who has discovered a new virus. He removes his sunglasses and puts on his bifocals. He bends over and examines Jalili up close, to determine whether he's still the same person he always was.

Shirin-khanom says slowly and sulkingly: "If you are sincere, then take his gag off."

Heydari bites his lip, leans back and stares into space. All the symptoms are there, all the symptoms of a strange illness.

"You're afraid of him, aren't you." says Shirin-khanom. Everyone's eyes are on Heydari. Everyone's ears await his voice.

Hashemi is kneeling next to Jalili's bed, fanning him. Jalili's father mumbles to himself: "Stupid boy; stupid, thoughtless boy."

Heydari stands up, his hands on his haunches. Everyone moves aside and makes way for him. He paces, goes toward the window, then walks back and looks at Jalili. He starts pacing again, stands next to the window and pulls the curtain aside. He doesn't move.

No one speaks.

From the hall comes the sound of something falling and breaking. Ammeh-jan Batul chants louder.

Asgari calls down through the furnace pipe, announcing that several people have turned into the street.

Someone's kicking at the door. It's Jalili's son. He's just returned from school. He bounds into the room and gulps down a half-empty glass of lemonade, wipes his inky hands on the tablecloth, spreads his notebooks in the middle of the room and gleefully shows everyone the large zero he's earned in arithmetic. Then he skips around the room and makes strange noises. He looks at his father's gagged mouth and laughs.

Ammeh-jan Batul curses him, from under her *chador,* saying: "He's just like his father, an ungodly little bastard."

Heydari starts pacing again. He comes over and stands next to Jalili's bed. "This man," he intones, "has always worried me. His unconventional ways always had me concerned. I could tell he wanted to cut himself off from us and go, but I always thought he would someday come to his senses."

Jalili's wife starts crying again. She blows her nose and sighs: "How happy we were!" she says. "We had everything, a house, a car, a child, social standing. . ."

"We should have tied him up before it ever came to this," says Jalili's brother.

Ammeh-jan Batul crawls closer. "These things are in a person's blood," she says. "He's been evil ever since he was a child. He wouldn't suckle at his mother's breast. Ever since he was young he's been different. His gaze would make a person shudder. "

There's a knock at the door. Everyone looks at Heydari.

Asgari yells down that they're not strangers. Hashemi runs out and opens the door. It's the cousins. They've brought a doctor and a box of *padashzadeh* candy. They're out of breath, hot and dusty, and they talk with everyone. They smell of fever and thirst. They bend over and kiss Jalili on the forehead. They shake hands with everyone, put a hand on Mrs. Jalili's shoulder, express their sympathy and inquire about the health of her respected father and her dear mother.

Hashemi moves up a chair for the doctor.

"Sir," says Heydari to the doctor, "allow me to explain the situation. I am his best friend."

Ammeh-jan Batul, like a monstrous black turtle, creeps closer. Her voice can be heard under the *chador*. "Let me explain," she says, "I know everything."

The cousins stand up and pay their respects to Ammeh-jan Batul. They inquire about the health of her sisters.

The doctor is elderly and has a kind face. His little blue eyes are full of inane laughter. His red lips constantly move. He looks at everyone and moves around in his chair.

Someone brings him some lemonade. He drinks it down and smacks his lips. He nods his head, and his puffy face shines. He's wearing red socks. He waves to Shirin-khanom. He looks at Jalili and smiles.

"Allow me to explain why we have bound and gagged him." says Jalili's wife.

"His wife has been hurt more than anyone." says Jalili's brother.

From outside come strange sounds, cheering, applause, screaming, honking and general commotion.

Asgari calls down through the furnace-pipe: "Don't worry; it's nothing. They're just carrying the lucky winners around on camels."[6]

Shouts and police whistles can be heard outside. Asgari calls down to say that the camels are stampeding.

The doctor is all excited, jumping up and down in his seat.

The neighbors take their leave, saying goodbye from the hallway. Their plates are empty.

The doctor begins his examination. He takes Jalili's pulse, looks under his eyelids, listens to his heart, looks inside his ears. He taps his stomach and his ribs, puts his ear to his chest, checks his blood pressure. He counts his toes, and taps his knee with a metal rod. He asks for his birthdate, occupation, place of work, and the names of his friends. "There's nothing wrong with him,"he says "Nothing."

"His head, doctor," says Jalili's father, "examine his head!"

"Ask why they've gagged him," says Shirin-khanom.

"We have no choice," says Jalili's wife. "If we take the gag off, he'll start talking."

Heydari says: "Our dear friend cannot distinguish right from wrong. He has gone astray in his choice of moral and spiritual values. It is our duty to guide him."

Jalili's wife weeps in silence. She sits next to her husband and kisses his bound hands. She caresses his hair and says: "It's all for his own sake, the poor dear. Otherwise what wife could bear to gag and tie up her husband? What father? What friend? "

Hashemi wipes his eyes with the back of his hand. Shirin-khanom mutters something to herself. The cousins sigh.

The doctor writes down some things quickly. Then he thinks. Then he says: "Yes. I see. I understand."

Jalili's father leans over to the doctor's ear and whispers: "Has he gone crazy?"

The doctor shakes his head.

Jalili's brother asks: "Is it psychological rebellion? "

The doctor smiles.

The cousins say: "Hopefully, God willing, he'll get well and make amends."

"Well, what is it? " asks Jalili's wife with impatience.

84

The doctor closes his notebook. Again the wrinkles on his face are full of that inane glee. "How can I say it?" he begins. "It's as if he's become a sparrow. A sparrow that wants to fly, but can't."

Jalili's father is frustrated. His cheeks are red. "Sir, what are you talking about?" he asks.

The doctor looks at him kindly. "That was a manner of speaking." he answers.

Jalili's father flies into a rage. He shouts and kicks the legs of Jalili's bed. "The hell he has! Do you mean to tell me that this grown-up fool, this son of mine, after leading an honorable and respectable life, has now turned into a sparrow!"

He runs out of breath, mouthing words with no sound, snorting. The cousins quickly take him by the arm and lead him out of the room. His arms and legs are flailing, and strange sounds, resembling a bunch of tin cans rattling together, come out of his throat.

Ammeh-jan Batul creeps closer. She's next to the doctor's chair. From under her *chador* she tells him: "Whatever it is, it started that day, the day we went to the cemetary. I saw it with my own eyes. He was standing in a corner and looking at the graves of the dead. His face was white and he was shaking."

"Yes," adds Jalili's brother, "sometimes he talked about death to me, too."

"What's all this talk?" says Heydari. "No one knows our dear friend here better than I. We grew up together. It is true, however, that our guilty friend always seemed to think too much, and look too much. But then he was young, and exposed to a thousand improper, turbulent desires."

"But I was the ideal wife for him!" says Jalili's wife. "I tried to change him, to set him straight, and I thought I'd succeeded!"

Heydari continues: "Yes. As I was saying. What was I saying? Well anyway, all the friends held him dear and admired him for how knowledgeable, intelligent and articulate he was. He was always the top student in all his classes. His wife is from one of the best families. We all envied him.

Please come and see for yourself. "

He gets up and points to Jalili's graduation picture on the wall. "This is he. How admirable! Look at that wholesome smile, at that face full of hope, at that expression. He's just bursting with youth and enthusiasm. Or take this picture here, in memory of the day of holy matrimony. He is a bit older here, of course, and he isn't smiling, but that's all right, one can't be smiling all the time. And here is his first picture with his firstborn child, between his respected father-in-law and his dear mother-in-law. And this is his latest picture. I believe it's at my birthday party. It isn't a good picture; that's the photographer's fault, otherwise our dear friend doesn't look like this."

The doctor looks closely at the picture, and says: "It's strange how much he's changed in this last picture. There's no resemblance to the first one."

Ammeh-jan Batul pokes at the doctor's leg: "Most nights he couldn't sleep." she says. "He'd get up and walk. I'd watch him from the roof. He looked as if something was hurting him. Something was wrong with him. He'd talk to himself and moan. And he'd take on a different shape at night. It was scary. He'd gradually turn into a wolf, a wolf out to tear everyone apart. He'd gnash his teeth and claw at the bark on the trees. I told them then, but they didn't listen; they didn't believe me."

"How could I have known? " says Jalili's wife. "As soon as I laid my head on the pillow, I'd fall asleep. I don't have psychic powers."

Shirin-khanom has tied the carpet fringe into knots. She pays no attention to anyone. She's pulled a piece of newspaper out from under the carpet and is reading it.

Azizi is still thinking about the sparrow that couldn't fly, that shouldn't fly.

"What should we do now? " asks Jalili's wife.

The doctor shuts his bag. He stands up and says: "He needs sleep, complete rest. It's nothing new. We've had a lot of these cases, a lot of sparrows like him. I'm prescribing some pills for him. Have him take three a day; they'll keep him groggy all day; then a shot at night; that'll keep him asleep all night. He'll be fine after a while. He won't move at all once you've untied him and removed the gag. Rest assured; today's drugs work miracles."

He shuts his bag and gets up to leave.

The cousins get up and accompany the doctor to the door.

"Give me the prescription," says Hashemi. "I'll go fill it."

"We should get him out of sight before someone shows up," says Heydari.

"Take him someplace far away," says Ammeh-jan Batul.

"How about the basement? " says Azizi.

Shirin-khanom gets up and leaves without saying goodbye.

Jalili's wife gathers up the leftover fruit from the plates.

Ammeh-jan Batul drags herself along the floor to the storage room.

Azizi wearily stands up and looks at his watch. He ties his shoelaces sadly, and says: "So everything's okay now. Or maybe it's not. What difference does it make? " He buttons his jacket and nods goodbye to everyone.

Asgari's and Azizi's voices can be heard in the street, as well as their footsteps as they hurry away.

Jalili's brother is looking for the key to the basement.

Heydari paces back and forth, calmly and silently. His head is low; he's tired and his eyes look yellow. His once abundant hair has thinned.

Jalili's wife is standing over her husband's bed. She comes up to him, leans over and pulls the sheet up over his face. She turns away, shrugs her shoulders and says: "What can I do? I can't bear to see him cry. "

---

1. In Iran sugar is also sold in large solid cones, which are then broken into lumps.

2. *Sowhan:* a special candy from the city of Qom, made with sesame and honey.

3. *Santur:* a traditional Persian instrument; one plays it by hitting the strings with narrow flat sticks.

4. Ammeh: paternal aunt.

87

5. A superstitious tradition to ward off evil spirits.
6. This follows a major soccer game.

9

Hashemi opened his eyes. Above his head were thick branches intertwined, full of strange birds chattering among the leaves. He listened. There was only the sound of the sea and the soft rustle of the wind on the sand and the chatter of the invisible birds as they jumped from one branch to another. He thought of Shirin-khanom and his heart twinged. He thought of her lisp, of her little round rump, of how she was knee-high to a grasshopper, and of her kindness that was for everyone. She was a fountain; she overflowed and was beautiful.

Heydari had asked: "Now who is this? Where did she come from? " Where *had* she come from? No one knew. Shirin-khanom had laughed. She'd pointed toward a place in the distance, to the sky, the trees, the neighbor's house, the fountain pool, the roof, this direction and that direction, and had said: "From there, from behind those trees, from in there, from way over that way, from those depths—what difference does it make? I'm here now. "

Anvari had said: "The family a woman comes from is important. Of all of us only Jalili's been lucky. "

Hashemi raised his head and looked around. Shirin-khanom

rested upon the waves, like a fish, like a mermaid.

He lay down again, and said in his heart: "My lady, my dear sweetheart, how wonderful it is that you exist, that you came. How good it is that the day begins with you, and ends with you. How wonderful to wake up and see you in front of me, next to me, behind me, here and there, to smell the fragrance of your hair, to hear your voice close by, to see your shoes next to the door, your clothes on the carpet, the shape of your body on the sheets, your fingerprints on the wall, everywhere. "

Heydari had said: "Come on now. What nonsense. That woman's no good for anything; she's not even a woman. One couldn't be happy with her. "

Anvari had said the same thing, only in a lower voice and a bit sheepishly.

The birds chased each other among the branches. The ground was warm and sticky.

Hashemi stretched out his hands and rubbed his fingers on the damp grass. He took several deep breaths, one after the other. He turned over and rubbed his face against the hot sand. "What wonderful sunshine!" he said to himself. "What wonderful smells! What a wonderful day! What a wonderful world! How wonderful that I am alive, that I exist. I wish everything could just stop and stay forever the way it is right now, with nothing coming, nothing going, nothing changing; I wish that everything could be, just be."

He thought of the future, of the day when Shirin-khanom wouldn't be there anymore, and his heart sank. He looked into the sky, into that passive source out of which time seemed to flow, like a molten substance, like a monstrous breath that swallowed everything away.

He pressed his palms and his knees against the earth, and whispered to himself: "But right now I'm here. This moment is mine; this smell, this sunshine, this beach and this sea are mine, and that's all that counts. It doesn't matter that I'm going to die someday. I don't care if all this is taken away from me some day. I have Shirin-khanom. I found her late, very late, when my life was half over. But she's here now, before me. "

He sat up. Shirin-khanom was floating behind the waves, far out. Hashemi looked at her yellow towel and white slippers in a heap under the tree, and chuckled. "She'll be coming back now. Then she'll wrap herself in her towel and lie down beside me. Then she'll lay her head against my chest, caress my face and blink at me. Then I'll pat her, and dry her off. I'll take her wet feet in my hands and say: 'My Shirinak, my butterfly, how good it is that you are with me, that you exist. If you weren't here, could this sunshine be so nice and warm? Would this grass be worthy of being green? '"

He was thirsty. He raised his canteen and drank. He took a cucumber out of the basket, peeled it and saved half for Shirin-khanom. "Is this me? " he whispered. "Is this really me? Maybe I'm dreaming. Maybe I'm just imagining it. " He ran his palm over his head, slowly and hesitantly. It was his own bald, dusty head. He touched his pimply forehead, his big, soft stomach, his heel and the painful corn on his toe. It was he, Hashem Hashemi, resident of 2 Shahrivar St., at the corner of Si-Metri Avenue and Heshmat-ol-Dowleh Street, forty-two years of age, art teacher. Yes, it was his own self, his own happy self, his own impossible self. But there he was, and who could deny it? Who could ignore his simple happiness? The small reason for it was right there, his sweet Shirin-khanom who splashed in the water and whose voice could be heard from afar. "What person, what force sent that woman to me? " he thought. "And why me? What did I ever do? What special aptitude did I show? None. I wasn't intelligent or handsome. I had no faith or religion. I never fought for anything or went after anything. I was just an art teacher and I had a friend called Mr. Heydari. Why me? I have no special mark, no great ancestry, no particular mission. Nothing at all."

He thought of his father, of his grandfather and of his great-grandfather. They weren't *seyyeds*[1] or divinely appointed; they had no special powers, and they didn't perform any miracles. His father had a pharmacy and made home remedies from flower seeds and plant roots. And there was his mother too, like all the other things that were just there, and no one thought of their ever not being there.

He thought of his friends, of Heydari who was his best friend, and of Anvari and Ahmadi and Mahdavi and Jalili. No, it wasn't because of them either. This happiness wasn't hereditary or acquired. It was a miracle. It was a unique occurrence—it was his.

He thought of himself, of his childhood. He couldn't recall. He was there among the rest of the children, among brothers and cousins and neighbors' children. Which one was he? He saw himself at the edge of the pool, in the alley, on the roof, in the schoolyard. And that was it. He had no childhood. He thought of his youth, of his studies and his work, of his twenties and his thirties and the years before and after. He saw himself here and there, but nowhere in particular. He knew that he had to have been twenty at some time, and thirty, since now he was forty-two. But when? His past was like a colorless substance diffused in the air; whenever he thought of a place, a mass of blurred shadows invaded his mind; but he couldn't remember anywhere as a "specific place": his past was an indistinct pattern formed by a bunch of days and nights and by a cloud of disconnected, scattered, unrelated moments.

It was only with Shirin-khanom that he'd started to have his own memories, his own past, his own place. He remembered every day, every place they had been, everything they had done, everything they had said. With Shirin-khanom, everything had begun, the first day, the second day, the third day and the days thereafter. Time had begun, time in terms of things, and time in terms of Hashemi. With Shirin-khanom certain things had come into existence: darkness and light, seasons, places, desires, fears, memories—and Hashemi himself. It was with Shirin-khanom that he had come to look at himself, to see himself, to realize that he was, had been, and one day would no longer be.

He ran his hands along the sand, and was amazed. How warm, soft and alive the earth was. He was surrounded by this brown substance. He'd never thought of the earth, of this smooth body that was always there beneath his feet, next to him, before his eyes: and now for the first time he was seeing it. He looked at the green branches over his head, at the little houses in the distance, at the sky, the sea, the wood, the grass and the rocks. He was seeing these things for the first time, and seeing himself among them. It was amazing. Where had they all been, and if they weren't there what would happen?

He stood up and waved at Shirin-khanom. He began to worry, stepped closer and called out to her. He waved her yellow towel from afar and shouted: "Hey, that's enough! Come on back! You've gone too far out. Come back!"

Asgari had said: "Yes, take her to the seaside for a few days. Then she'll be better again. " Heydari had said: "She's just trying to get attention. She's spoiled. Don't pay any attention to her." Anvari had said: "Maybe she's sick. Maybe she's in some kind of pain. Take her to the doctor."

Hashemi had looked into Shirin-khanom's feverish and bewildered eyes, and asked: "What's happened, sweetheart? Why do you sit in a corner and sigh? Why are you suddenly so aloof from everyone? Why did you take off your ruby earrings and throw your bangles to the ground?"

Shirin-khanom bobbed behind the waves; only her head was above the water. Hashemi said to himself: "'Good old Hashemi, how is it that destiny has been so agreeable to you? How is it that all at once you had all of this, all this littleness that to you is limitless? What did you do? Nothing. ' But one day, without warning, unexpectedly, I looked out and saw someone sitting in front of me. Someone who's somehow related to me, who talks to me, listens to my voice, takes my hand and calls my name. I looked at her. Her eyes twinkled. She was little and round and plump. She cooed. She sparkled, like glass, like a bubble above the water. I saw her under my blankets, under my pillow, in the folds of the sheets. I saw her ringlets next to my bald head, and her pink thumb, no bigger than the seed of a grape, next to my big hairy black thumb. I saw her everywhere. Wherever I looked, in all the rooms, in the hallway, in the bathroom, among the trees, here and there. Wherever I went she was there, wherever I was. I'd say:

'Shirinak, are you some kind of genie? Maybe you're a fairy princess. How is it that you're everywhere I go? You're everywhere! Do you just cast a spell and appear? Maybe you've come from the invisible world!' She'd laugh and her teeth would shine. She'd lie down beside me and caress my hair. She'd put her head on my chest and hum a song. I'd say: 'Little lady, you were just now out hanging clothes on the line, you were in the kitchen cooking, I could hear your voice in the street, you were sleeping under the *korsi*.[2] How can you be here?' She'd rest her chin on her hands and just look at me. I knew she had to be here, and everywhere, just like light, like air, like something diffuse and abundant and open, better and more necessary than all of those. I wish she were here right now. I wish her hand were in mine and we were talking together.''

Azizi had said: "Shirin-khanom, what's the matter? Why have you become so quiet? Are you upset over your lost dove? The one that took off and flew away? Is that it?''

Heydari had said: "I'm going crazy. Why does she look at me that way every time she sees me? As if it's my fault she doesn't feel well."

Hashemi got up and stepped closer, then closer still. The sea poured onto the beach and then receded. The sea was restless. The birds shrieked. The birds in the branches were in a frenzy. He bent over and splashed some sea water onto his face; it was salty and it burned his eyes. He looked down at the worm crawling next to his foot, and called out to Shirin-khanom. "My sweet Shirin, my beautiful," he whispered, "I adore you. Are you a balloon, or a cloud, or a puff of air, that you float so lightly on the water? My little rubber ball, how is it that your feet never touch the ground? Remember our wedding night? You sat on the edge of the chair and only the tip of your tiny toe touched the carpet. And remember when I took you on a trip? Your feet didn't reach the floor of the bus. The other passengers had noticed and laughed. The Friends had laughed too. 'Weren't there enough women to go around?' they'd said. 'Who is this? She's cross-eyed, she's dumb, she's no bigger than an ant. Why is she always laughing for no reason? Why is she happy for no reason? Why does she take everyone's hand and act so nice to everyone? She's an embarrassment. No one has taught her to how to behave with people. She has no cunning. She's not educated. Where are her papers? Who is her family? No, she's nothing a man could be happy with. No way. ' Heydari had said: 'My foolish friend, why did you go and fall in love without discussing it with me? You know you don't understand these things. This isn't what love is. '"

Hashemi squeezed his eyes shut and put his hand to his forehead. The sun beat right down through him. He was blacking out. The sea was full of gold sequins that flashed blindingly before his eyes. He felt as if he were melting like a piece of wax, and that his arms and legs were taking root in the sand, like a creeping vine.

The birds were swarming from branch to branch. Hashemi picked up a rock and threw it at them. His head was full of strange noises, the sound of the sea, of the birds, of the wind. He went back under the tree and picked up Shirin's towel. Shirin-khanom's clothes were lying farther over in a heap. Her shoes were there too. Everything was as usual. What wonderful sunshine. What a wonderful day. What a wonderful sea. He picked up Shirin-khanom's clothes and shook them out. He laughed. He held her skirt up to his waist and put his hands into her slippers, and laughed louder. He looked up and searched for Shirin-khanom. The sea was calm and grey; it breathed gently, as if its anxiety had subsided.

"My butterfly," whispered Hashemi, "my Shirinak, where are you?" He crawled closer, then closer still. The water came up to his knees. He looked around him, at the far end of the beach, at the sea. "Maybe behind the bushes." he said. "Maybe she's behind the dunes. She must be around here somewhere."

Heydari had said: "A man doesn't find happiness just like that, with no planning and organizing. That kind of thing takes skill."

Anvari had said: "The monster came and took away my friend. And took him so easily!" Very easily, in an instant, in the blink of an eye.

Hashemi looked at his trembling hands, at his skin covered with goosebumps, at his knees that had grown weak. The sun beat down on his head. Something like a stubborn insect buzzed next to his ear. He went back under the tree and looked at the scattered array of his footprints on the sand. "She's right around here. " he said. "She must be around nearby."

The sea watched him, unfamiliar and indifferent. It didn't even move. It was peaceful and sated, as if it had just consumated a passionate embrace.

He ran toward the sea, and stopped. He looked behind him and laughed. He turned around and retraced his steps. "She's playing a trick on me," he mumbled. "She wants to give me a hard time. I know. I'm sure. " He sat down and listened, frightened, to the silence behind the dunes, to the silence that was everywhere, in the sky and over the sea. It seemed to him that everything, the wilderness and the sky and even the pebbles, was looking at him. "She isn't here:" he said to himself. "My Shirinak really isn't here."

He couldn't believe it. It was all a bad dream. He would wake up and find Shirin-khanom sitting next to him. He lay down, hurriedly closed his eyes and waited for someone to wake him from this nightmare. But something other than sleep lurked in the back of his mind, something that was aware, that knew, and that warned him, something that realized that all this was a game and that the truth was something else.

So it was true: this tragedy that he'd smelled from far away was his. He sat up. His body was heavy. The wind against his face was rough and hot and sticky. It clung to his body and stayed there, like a weight.

"She's still there." he said to himself. "She's there. She'll be right back. She'll be coming any minute."

Something like Shirin-khanom's hand moved on the water far out. He fell on his hands and knees, and crawled, closer and closer. Shirin-khanom's towel lay in his path. He picked it up, held it tightly and bit onto a corner. He wanted to drive away that noxious enemy that buzzed behind his head, that undying awareness, that perpetual feeling of reality. He banged his fist on the ground and rubbed his face in the sand. "It's impossible," he said, "impossible!" And he laughed, louder, faster, and more sadly. He tried to sing, to count the cloud wisps in the sky. He tried to talk, to think, to remember—he even tried to die. It was no use. He knew that dreadful moment had come, that unreality whose chance of becoming a reality had always beckoned, which he'd never heeded and which was now here—tangible and real. An impossibility that had so easily become possible.

Someone was walking along the beach, singing, away from the water. Hashemi thought of calling him, running after him, asking for help. The two of them would be strong enough to tackle the sea. They'd find Shirin-khanom, hold her up, take her back from the sea.

He opened his mouth and tried to shout. His voice wouldn't come out. He tried to wave; he tried to run after the man; he tried to do something. He sat up and stared into the sea, transfixed. "It is my inalienable right," he said to himself. "She was given to me. She came to me, like a dove of good fortune, like a winning lottery ticket. I'll take her in my arms. I'll hold her tight. I'll say: 'Sweetheart, you can't not be; you're forever, you're needed, you're more important than anything. You'll come back. You have to come back. You can't help it.'"

The sun moved slowly towards the sea. The birds slept. Not a sound could be heard, except Hashemi murmuring to himself: "What a wonderful day. What a wonderful sea. What a wonderful world."

---

1. Descendants of the prophet Mohammad, by his daughter Fatimah and her husband Ali.

2. *Korsi*: a traditional Iranian heating system, consisting of a tray of hot coals placed under a low table, which is covered by a large quilt. People sit around the *korsi* with their legs under the quilt for warmth.

10

"Old man, see how you were fooled? "

That's Heydari's voice. He's here, sitting next to me. His eyes shine in the dark. I turn over, and put my head under the blanket. "Old man, listen to me. It's for your own good. " His head is on the pillow next to mine. His hair smells of coconut oil and raw chickpeas, as usual. "Heydari-jan," I tell him, are you still worrying about your hair and about washing your hands? About your fillings and your pimples? "

He's sitting in the middle of my head, walking behind my eyelids. All my memories are filled with his presence. I can see him, sitting in the sun; he's rubbed egg yolk on his hair and wrapped his head in a plastic bag. He was always thinking of his hair, his thin hair that was slowly falling out.

We'd go hiking together. He'd always bring boiled water and cooked vegetables. He'd sit at the edge of the stream and wash the fruit with soap. Then he'd brush his teeth and gargle, then dust off his shoes and laugh. When he caught typhoid he was only forty years old. We'd just celebrated his birthday. We laughed and said: "How can someone who's forty years old catch typhoid? " And someone like him! We couldn't believe

98

it. We were at his bedside; Hashemi had brought him some herbal remedies, with syrups and brews made of leaves, roots and seeds. We realized that he was dying. We couldn't believe it. We couldn't accept it. We'd forgotten all about death. It didn't apply to us. Manizheh was there too. "This is just a game." she said. "How could such a thing happen? How could it be possible? " We didn't believe it either. We had known a Heydari whose death was impossible. There was something about his rosy complexion and white teeth that refuted his mortality. Only his hair was falling out. But we were confident about that as well; we knew it would grow back again. He too was confident. He'd found the cure for it. "Friends," he'd said, "trust me. In the end victory will be ours."

We looked at him, and saw that something within us as well was coming to an end.

"It'll be our turn too." said Hashemi. But when? If only we knew. If only we knew when that accursed moment would come. Heydari laughed at our simple-mindedness. "I'm a healthy man." he said. "I am steel. Steel doesn't rust. Steel is forever steel." He ran his hand over his head and looked at us with fear. "It'll grow back;" he said, "believe me. I take good care of my hair. I keep track of each one that falls, and each one that grows in. I've figured out the way. It takes patience and perseverence. " He plucked all the hairs from the sheet and pillowcase. He counted them, and placed them side by side in the fold of a newspaper. He did keep track of them. And we kept track of him. Heydari was pleased. "Perfect!" he said. "Just great! More are growing in, more than yesterday. My hair's growing back. " He took my hand and looked at me: "See," he said, "I was right. See how everything has a way? Didn't I say in the end victory would be mine? " He was happy; and then he died.

Azizi and I were left. We'd sit on the sidewalk bench and look at the empty street, at a passerby or an occasional face in a window. We'd remember Heydari too, his thick hair that fell out in tufts and the thin skin on his hands, and we'd recall things we were gradually beginning to forget. Sometimes we'd talk. We'd talk about the same things we'd talked about over and over again. I'd talk about Manizheh and he'd talk about his son.

When she divorced me and left, I still loved her. Her leaving me was a tragedy, one that I'd always anticipated deep in my heart, and I knew that one day she'd catch me unaware. The friends told me: "It doesn't matter. Start over again. Find another wife. Do something else. " They said: "It's your own fault. Why did you let her go? " She wanted children. I understood. She was sad. "Don't think it's that I'm not happy with you. " she said. "But what am I to do? I can't help it. I can't control it. I have no other choice." She packed her things, and cried. I understood. I knew. I recognized her look; it was the same look Heydari had the day he was dying, in the last moment when he turned and looked at me. He had sensed the presence of death, the presence of that strange darkness, of that sucking void that had opened up to swallow him.

"Manizheh-jan," I said. "I wish you weren't leaving. " She left. She married the neighborhood policeman, the one who directed traffic at the corner. I saw her once. She had three children. She laughed; her teeth had fallen out, and she'd grown fat. She smelled like the neighborhood policeman. She was a stranger. "My husband's a good man. " she said. "His only problem is that his feet smell." She picked up her daughter and kissed her. Her hands were covered with white blotches. "Do you still sleep with the window open at night? " she asked me. "Do you still talk in your sleep? How are the jasmine plants? Do they still bloom? Are you still such a worrywart? Do you still smoke three packs a day?"

"What good times we had together," she said. "How we used to laugh!" She showed me her son. She caressed his curly forelock, buttoned his collar and pinched his cheek. She was among her children, a unit, a complete circle.

"Yeah," said Azizi, "sure, I have a son, but what good has it done me? He went off to study abroad and he's never come back. He was supposed to become an engineer or a doctor, but he never did. He ended up staying there. Became a waiter, married some foreign woman, and now he's got himself a red-haired, blue-eyed kid. He's forgotten that I'm here waiting, for the doctor, for the engineer, for my son."

"I wish we could start all over again," I said. "What could we do?" said Azizi. "We'd still end up right here, with the same wish. There's no other way for us. We're little people." He went on. "Where could we go conquer? What could we do? All there is is eating and sleeping and a house and a savings account, and occasionally some good clean fun. A modest lot. But it wasn't bad; we should be grateful. We're better off than a lot of people, and farther ahead. And we haven't had such a bad life, in all fairness. Sometimes we laughed—maybe it wasn't heartfelt, but still, it wasn't bad. Remember the nights we'd all get together and get drunk? We'd talk, and then doze off in a corner. It wasn't bad. What else did you expect?"

Gradually we stopped talking. We'd become hard of hearing. We no longer heard what the other said. So we just sat together and waited for the time to pass. Just being together was good; we weren't alone. What did we think about? We knew that one of us would someday sit on this bench and think of the other who was no longer there. Which one of us would it be? It was so strange. We had always been on the move, always waiting for the next day; and now there was only the past. Time no longer unfolded; we had come to know it, and now its existence was only a memory. We seemed to be caught in a temporary pause, an empty pause in which nothing happened, and nothing would happen after that. We were only a step away from that eternal void. We both knew what we were thinking about. We could tell whenever we caught each other's eye, when we greeted each other, and when we made plans to meet the next day.

"You've changed so much!" said Manizheh. "You've grown so thin and old! Are you ill, God forbid? What's the matter? Why are you limping? Are you eating regularly? Do you feel all right?" She showed me her children: "He's the oldest. He's in the fifth grade, at the top of his class. This is my daughter. Her name is Shapareh. She's cute and winsome. And here's the last of the bunch: he's naughty, a real charmer."

I looked at her swollen fingertips. "I sew." she said. "I make clothes for the neighbors. What can I do? There are so many things you have to buy for these kids. It's for them I work so hard. I live for them."

Why did she want children so much? We had a good life, and we passed the time pleasantly.

I wish I could go out. I feel the urge to go out and walk under the snow. But it's cold, and this snow isn't the usual kind of snow; it's freezing and deadly. That kind of urge has to wait for summertime.

Manizheh said: "But you can't stand the heat. You get dizzy and feel sick; you get all kinds of aches and pains. So why are you always anxious for summertime?"

I was supposed to go with Asgari. God knows where. What difference did it make? Wherever we went would have been better than here. There's nothing left here. Nothing. We should have gone. We should have taken the risk. We should have done something, something besides waiting, besides fearing, besides counting and measuring. Asgari said: "This land is sterile; it'll make our roots wither. Let's get up and go. Maybe we can put roots down somewhere else, be free and fly. Here we're just dying. We're growing old."

Azizi said: "I'm not going. I'm waiting for my son, His Excellency the Waiter."

"We've got to go before it's too late," said Asgari. He never gave up the thought of this journey. From when we were children he talked about it, throughout our youth he dreamed about it. He'd say to me: "This city is mean and greedy. It stabs you in the back. It's vile. It's robbing us of our youth, and tricking us. Come on, let's go!" But we didn't. None of us went. Why not? It was Asgari's fault. It was his mother's fault, for being old and bedridden. It was Heydari's fault for bringing us to our senses. Or maybe it wasn't anyone's fault. We had no choice but to stay.

Anvari said: "Asgari-jan, are you going to waste your whole life taking care of your crippled mother? "

He sat next to his mother. He massaged her legs, fanned her, combed her hair. "She still remembers her ruby earrings. " he said. "I tried to take them off, but she wouldn't let me. She buried her head in the pillow and wailed."

He went and brought her mother's necklace and fastened it around her neck. Then he brought out her rings and put them on her fingers one by one. He arranged her white, matted hair in ringlets on the pillow. He lay her satin dress over her, and sat and looked at her.

"So what about our journey? " I said.

"You go ahead. " he said. "You're not tied to anyone. Why are you standing there next to me wasting your time? Go. Before it's too late. While there's still time."

"Time for what? " I asked. "For happiness?"

"Yes." he answered.

It was Manizheh's fault. If she hadn't left me everything would have been different. Or Heydari, for instance. Why did he die so soon? How could I be happy without them? Without those others that I loved. Or didn't love. What difference does it make? It was with them that I felt alive.

Asgari said: "Why do you go on about Heydari? Heydari's death doesn't mean the end for you. To hell with Heydari. You're still alive. You have time. Why are you mourning?"

I said: "I'll wait till summer comes."

"To hell with summer!" he answered. "Summer is for the trees and the flowers. Your time has nothing to do with them."

I told Asgari: "You'll get that disease too. You're going to end up like your mother, crippled and blind and mute. " He laughed and nodded. He was holding his mother's hand. He knew. "This is a kind of journey," he said, "my journey. " I wanted to help him, to stay with his mother. He wouldn't let me. It wasn't my responsibility, nor my place. We went to see him, with the Friends. We knocked on his door; he didn't answer. We called to him from the window; he didn't open the door. What could we do? He wanted it that way.

103

"It's just as well you didn't go off with Asgari." said Azizi. "You can complain all you like, but it's safe and secure here. We have a house and a street and a few trees. We have a policeman who blows his whistle at night, and a clinic. Wherever you go it would be the same."

Heydari said: "The secret of success is in our unity. Let me protect that unity. Give me all your money so I can buy land for you."

We agreed to. We told each other we'd be rich some day. We sat and waited, until that summer, until the summer after, until the summer after all the summers.

I want to go to sleep. I don't want to think about anything anymore. I'm tired. How can I express it? I'm old. There's a rat gnawing at the tip of the mattress. There used to be a cat around here; I'd hear its voice. Since the weather's turned cold it hasn't come around. Tomorrow I'll go out and buy some traps. And I'll bring over the neighbor's cat. As Heydari used to say: "Every problem has a solution. It takes patience and perseverence. In the end, victory will be ours."